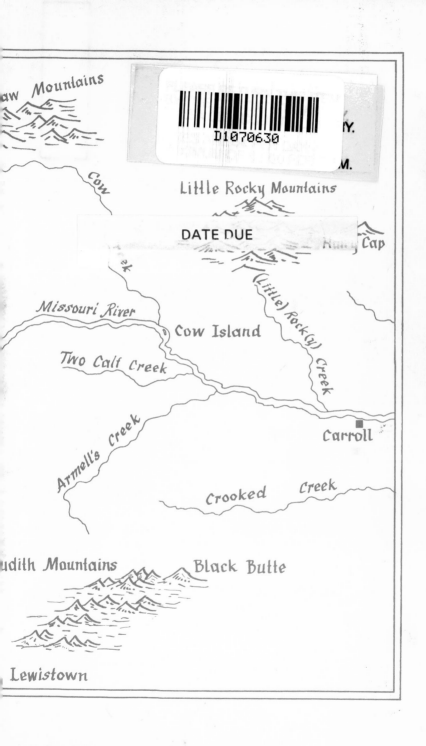

aw Mountains

Little Rocky Mountains

Cap

Missouri River

Cow Island

Two Calf Creek

(Little) Rocky Creek

Armell's Creek

Carroll

Crooked Creek

udith Mountains   Black Butte

Lewistown

Floating on the Missouri

by
James Willard Schultz
(Apikuni)

Edited by
Eugene Lee Silliman

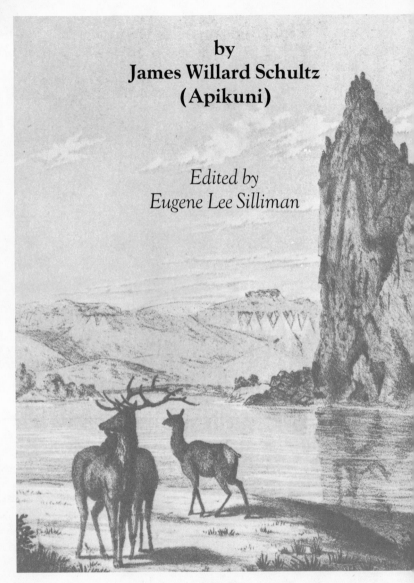

Citadel Rock,
from A. E. Mathews' *Pencil Sketches of Montana, 1868*,
courtesy Montana Historical Society

Floating on the Missouri

University of Oklahoma Press
Norman

Library of Congress Cataloging in Publication Data

Schultz, James Willard, 1859–1947.
  Floating on the Missouri.

  Includes bibliographical references.
      1.   Missouri River – Description and travel.
2.   Missouri Valley – Description and travel.
3.   Boats and boating – Missouri River.   4.   Schultz,
James Willard, 1859–1947.   I.   Silliman, Eugene Lee.
II.   Title.
F598.S38   1979   917.86'1   79–4741
ISBN 0–8061–1588–2

. . . *I reckon I got to light out for the Territory ahead of the rest, because Aunt Sally she's going to adopt me and civilize me, and I can't stand it. I been there before.*

Huck Finn

INTRODUCTION

I N this brief introduction to *Floating on the Missouri*, it
seems desirable, for today's readers, to say something
about the author, something about the setting, and something about the book.

About the Author

A visit with relatives in St. Louis first brought James Willard
Schultz in contact with men from the Far West. As a youngster
in New York he had developed a strong love of outdoor life.
The restless and difficult adolescent—he had been expelled
from military school—was excited by tales of adventure among
Indians and buffaloes.

And so in the spring of 1877 the seventeen-year-old Schultz
boarded the steamer *Benton* headed up the Missouri River
for Montana Territory:

*I saw every foot of the Missouri's shores, 2,600 miles, which
lay between the Mississippi and our destination, Fort Benton,
at the head of navigation. I saw the beautiful groves and
rolling green slopes of the lower river, the weird "badlands"
above them, and the picturesque cliffs and walls of sandstone, carved into all sorts of fantastic shapes and forms by
wind and storm, which are the features of the upper portion
of the navigable part of the river . . . After we entered buffalo
country there were many places which I passed with regret;
I wanted to stop off and explore them.**

In Fort Benton the lad was befriended by Joseph Kipp, an
experienced Indian trader who followed the Blackfoot In-

*James Willard Schultz, *My Life as an Indian* (New York, Houghton
Mifflin Co., 1914), 4–5.

vii

dians across the central Montana plains. Schultz became intimately acquainted with the tribe and its domain, taking part in its buffalo hunts and war parties. Apikuni, or Far-Off-White-Robe, as the Blackfeet called Schultz, married a young Indian woman in 1879. Natahki (Fine Shield Woman) bore him his only child, Hart Merriam Schultz, known as the noted Indian artist Lone Wolf. Upon the extermination of the buffalo herds the family settled on the Blackfoot reservation near Browning, Montana. An indifferent rancher, Schultz enjoyed guiding hunting parties into the nearby Rocky Mountains. He also spent much time talking with and listening to the venerable Blackfoot warriors as they recalled their past adventures.

Among Schultz's regular clients was George Bird Grinnell, an eminent naturalist and student of Indian history. Together they explored the rugged glaciated mountains west of the reservation. The beauty of the majestic peaks and the placid mountain lakes inspired Grinnell to campaign to preserve the area. Schultz assisted him by writing magazine articles and reports. Legislation finally established the area as Glacier National Park. It is appropriate that some natural features in the park honor these two men: Grinnell Glacier, Grinnell Falls, Grinnell Lake, and Mount Grinnell; Appekunny Mountain, Appekunny Creek, and Appekunny Falls ("Appekunny" is Grinnell's spelling of Schultz's Indian name). The names Gunsight Pass and Fusillade Mountain commemorate an 1890 hunting expedition by the pair. Many other mountain peaks bear the Blackfoot Indian names recommended by Schultz.

As editor of the popular outdoor magazine *Forest and Stream*, Grinnell encouraged his friend to submit stories of the Blackfoot adventures he often told at the campfire. Thus began a twenty-year writing period in which Schultz treated the readers of *Forest and Stream* to his personal view of Indian and frontier life. Grinnell borrowed some of Schultz's material to publish *Blackfoot Lodge Tales* in 1892. Most of

Schultz's stories appeared under a pseudonym or under his Indian name; even many of the characters in his stories were renamed. The probable explanation was given in a 1906 story about Joseph Kipp: "He still lives; and as I may in the course of this story tell some of the things we did together, for which we are now both truly sorry, I will not give his right name." (They had occasionally cheated the Indians.)

In the fall of 1901, Schultz and his wife decided to float the Missouri River. During the trip Natahki complained of pains in her fingers. They thought it was rheumatism, but the pain spread and worsened. After the trip their doctor diagnosed a terminal heart condition. The end is described in the last paragraph of *My Life as an Indian:* "For eleven months we all did what we could, and then one day, my faithful, loving, tender-hearted little woman passed away, and left me. By day I think of her, at night I dream of her. I wish that I had that faith which teaches us that we will meet again on the other shore. But all looks very dark to me." It was a blow from which Schultz never fully recovered.

The next year Schultz and a client were arrested for killing game illegally. After the case was continued several times, Schultz moved to the West Coast. (The charges against him were dropped in 1915.) In California, Schultz was a publicity agent for an oil company and later a literary critic for the *Los Angeles Times.* While he held these jobs, he continued to write for *Forest and Stream.* His efforts for Grinnell reached their zenith in 1906 with the serialized publication of his autobiography, *My Life as an Indian.* It was shortly thereafter published in book form. Throughout its pages is expressed a love for a land and its irretrievable past: "Wide, brown plains, distant, slender, flat topped buttes; still more distant giant mountains, blue-sided, sharp-peaked, snow-capped; odour of sage and smoke of camp fire; thunder of ten thousand buffalo hoofs over the hard, dry ground; long-drawn, melancholy howl of wolves breaking the silence of night, how I love you all!"

Most of the books and articles read by the general public in those days portrayed Indians as cruel savages, insensible primitives, indolent wards, or necessary victims of manifest destiny. In the introduction to *My Life as an Indian*, Grinnell summarized well Schultz's profound understanding of and respect for the Indian:

The author has penetrated the veil of racial indifference and misunderstanding and has got close to the heart of the people about whom he writes. Such an intimate revelation of the domestic life of the Indians has never before been written. The sympathetic insight everywhere evident is everywhere convincing. We feel that the men and the women portrayed are men and women of actual living existence. And while in the lodges on the Marias the elemental passions have fuller and franker sway, we recognize in the Blackfoot as here revealed a creature of common humanity like our own. His are the same loves and hates and hopes and fears. The motives which move him are those which move us.

The wide acclaim *My Life as an Indian* has received over the many years since its publication is a testimony to its excellence.

Spurred by the success of his first book, Schultz began writing in earnest. Most of his work was published serially in youth magazines such as the *American Boy, Boy's Life,* and *St. Nicholas* before being issued in book form. Between 1906 and 1940 he wrote thirty-seven books, fiction and nonfiction. Though they were most popular among young people, the books have enduring interest to readers of all ages wishing to understand the thoughts, feelings, and habits of the Plains Indian.

Nearly every summer from 1915 on, Schultz returned to the Blackfoot reservation to visit with old friends and to acquire new information and inspiration for future books. He also retreated to a cabin in the White Mountains of eastern California, where he became acquainted with the Hopi Indians. Schultz wrote *In The Great Apache Forest* when he learned that the Hopis' Indian agent and reservation missionaries were trying to suppress their religion. The letters of protest that flowed in as a result of this book helped persuade the commissioner of Indian Affairs to rescind the ban on Indian ceremonies. Schultz also spearheaded an organization of influential persons whose purpose was to protect the rights of the American Indian and to reform the policies of the Bureau of Indian Affairs.

In 1927, Schultz became acquainted with Jessie Donaldson, a young English teacher at Montana State College who had developed an interest in his writing. The two collaborated in the writing of *The Sun God's Children* before their marriage in 1931.* Jessie took a genuine interest in her husband's vocation, and was readily accepted by Schultz's Blackfoot friends. During the Depression they lived on the Blackfoot reservation, where Jessie developed a craft program to revive the nearly lost handwork skills of the Indians. After their move to Fort Washakie, Wyoming, in 1940, sickness and old age hampered Schultz's efforts to write. His end was best described by Jessie: "I should have known that his time had come. The Blackfeet always said that it is sure to storm when a chief passes. On the 11th of June, 1947, four inches of snow fell on the Wind River Reservation in Wyoming. Apikuni passed away that afternoon."†

---

*Jessie Donaldson Schultz, *Adventuresome, Amazing Apikuni*, Montana Heritage Series No. 12 (Montana Historical Society, 1961), 15.

†Schultz had married Celia B. Hawkins in 1907. Their incompatibility was soon apparent, and the marriage finally ended in divorce.

Floating on the Missouri
About the Setting

During a time period from 600 million to 60 million years ago present-day Montana was repeatedly inundated by shallow seas from the east. The waters laid down layers of sediments thousands of feet thick. In central Montana—the area pertinent to this book—these loosely consolidated deposits were mainly sandstone, limestone, and soft clays. About 60 million years ago a great uplift began, roughly centered on the Continental Divide. Some of the streams coursing eastward joined together to form the Missouri River. The scant rainfall and consequent lack of vegetation permitted the severe erosion of the loose material during the infrequent but violent summer rainstorms. The result was a labyrinth of steep gullies stretching for miles on both sides of the Missouri and up its tributaries. The French explorers called them *mauvaises terres,* meaning "bad lands."

The Missouri River badlands, or breaks, were well named. They were indeed "bad" to anyone attempting to traverse them. The steep gradients, the scarcity of water, the alkalinity of what little water could be found, the confusing mazes, and the nearly unbearable summer heat combined to make the badlands a region to avoid. One might travel up the Missouri through them, but not into them. As a final impediment, the clayish soils when wet turned into the notorious Missouri River gumbo—a greasy, sticky, endless mass of mud through which it is nearly impossible to move. Even today motorized vehicles halt when the badlands become wet. But for all its inhospitableness, the area is incredibly beautiful, as Schultz's narrative shows. The ocher, mauve, and gray soils; the silver sagebrush; the green ponderosa pines; the cool olive willow banks, the deep-blue distant buttes; and the azure sky paint a colorful scene. The twisted, seemingly desolate landscape is beautiful simply because it is natural.

Introduction

Perhaps the best-known portion of the Missouri River in central Montana is the white-cliffs region between Fort Benton and Judith River, where are found sculpturelike formations of white limestone and towering buttresses of dark volcanic intrusions. In 1833 the German Prince Maximilian zu Wied excitedly recorded: "Here, on both sides of the river, the most strange forms are seen, and you may fancy that you see colonnades, small round pillars with large globes or a flat slab at the top, little towers, pulpits, organs with their pipes, old ruins, fortresses, castles, churches, with pointed towers, &c. &c., almost every mountain bearing on its summit some similar structure." Some of the more imposing landmarks were given fanciful names: Citadel Rock, Hole-in-the-Wall, Steamboat Rock, Eagle Rock.

The history of the Missouri River reflects the history of Montana in the nineteenth century. Upon its waters and banks was played the drama of exploration, fur trading, gold fever, and Indian fighting. The first white men known to ascend the mighty river were the members of the Lewis and Clark Expedition. Both Meriwether Lewis and William Clark were keen observers, and in 1804 they recorded vivid and alluring descriptions of the Upper Missouri. They carefully noted the flora, fauna, and physiography of this strange land; they named many of the natural features; and they were enchanted by it. "The hills and river clifts which we passed today exhibit a most romantic appearance." To think of the Missouri River is to think of Lewis and Clark.

Soon after the expedition returned, word spread that the headwaters of the Missouri were rich in furs. For the next thirty years fur trappers and traders—Manuel Lisa, Andrew Henry, and George Drouillard, among others—toiled up the river in keelboats to exploit the riches of the Northern Rockies. The Indian traders established posts on the river from which to conduct their operations—Fort McKenzie, Fort Benton, Fort Chardon, Fort Union, and others.

In the 1860's gold was discovered in the mountains of the river's headwaters. By steamboat and mackinaw came thousands of crazed gold seekers bound for the placer diggings of Virginia City and Last Chance Gulch. This traffic of men and supplies up the Missouri marked the height of activity on the river. Yet even after the gold fever subsided, the settlements that became rooted in the western Montana valleys were supplied by Missouri River steamers. The last flurry of action came with the Indian wars of the 1870's. Steamboats were busy ferrying soldiers and supplies to fight the Sioux, Cheyennes, and Nez Perces. When the Northern Pacific Railroad finally reached Montana in 1881, all became peaceful on the Missouri. For nearly three quarters of a century the river had been the lifeline of Montana.

For the past hundred years the river has been less significant to life in Montana. When the river was no longer traveled, people drifted away from the region. The homesteaders who flooded the state in the beginning of the twentieth century shunned the arid, unfertile river breaks. A few cattle ranchers grazed their herds on the river's flanks, disturbing it little. With such inconsequential attention, the Missouri River breaks remained mostly unmolested. For that reason one can still today run Deadman Rapids, look up the looming hulk of La Barge Rock, camp on Cow Island, walk in the trenches of Camp Cooke, and appreciate a land nearly as virgin as the day Lewis and Clark first saw it.

On the other hand, whenever someone wanted to use or change the river, few were concerned. In the 1930's the federal government constructed the Fort Peck Dam and Reservoir. While it provided flood control and power generation, it also eliminated the unique features of 130 miles of wild river. Today's adventurer cannot retrace half of Schultz's trip

—or Lewis and Clark's either—on a free-flowing river. As a National Park Service paper put it, "The land which was once the river's verge is drowned-out, and the events of a former time take on the quality of a myth, forever beyond the affirmation of the eye." The portion of the river between Fort Benton and the Fort Peck Reservoir is the last unspoiled free-flowing section of the Missouri. Will we use it to turn more generators or preserve it as a historical and natural entity? I think I know how James Willard Schultz would have felt.

About the Book

When, in the fall of 1901, Schultz and Natahki decided to float the Missouri, they longed to see again the river and its tortured breaks, to visit the scenes of their earlier adventures, to recall the memory of their happiest days. "The shifting, boiling flood, the weird cliffs, the beautifully timbered, silent valley had a peculiar fascination for us such as no place in the great mountains possessed."

The description of their last trip and all the memories it evoked are the subject of *Floating on the Missouri*. It was first published in twelve installments, or chapters, in *Forest and Stream*, between February 15 and May 24, 1902, and has not, until now, been brought together and published in book form. The text, as presented here, is essentially as it appeared originally, with a few and minor editorial changes, and it should be mentioned that Schultz's spellings of proper names may differ from those used today. Some long paragraphs have been divided for the ease of reading, and a few editorial notes have been added to help document or explain certain passages.

Today the story of this remarkable trip is virtually unknown, except to a handful of Schultz fans, but it is a small jewel, a literary and descriptive gem that deserves to be in print and available.

Floating on the Missouri

It is almost as if Huck Finn, after completing one river trip, went west, grew up, and took another. The river affords a means for Schultz to describe places, conditions, people, and events along it, then and earlier, to weave in Indian mythology, to comment on the beauty of nature, and to speculate on the fate of it all in the face of advancing civilization. What he has to say about life along the river is from the past, but with something of interest for us today.

Eugene Lee Silliman

Deer Lodge, Montana

Floating on the Missouri

I

AT last our dreams were about to be realized. We had long planned a trip down the Missouri from Fort Benton, the head of navigation, to—well, some point to be determined upon later, and here we were, boat loaded, ready to embark. The boat we had named the "Good Shield," which is the English of our better half's Indian name, was just a plain, sharp-bowed, flat-bottomed skiff, some nineteen-feet long and of five-feet beam. Not exactly a thing of beauty, but staunch, light of draft, and serviceable. It held our tent, stove, bedding, clothing, guns and ammunition, provisions for a month or so, and still there was room for more.

So impatient were we to be off that we had loaded up by the light of a lantern. But now the eastern sky was streaked with crimson, and it was quite light enough to see the channel. The swift current was gently tossing and swaying our craft, as if to say: "Come, why tarry? Cast loose and I will bear you swiftly into the land of your dreams." Well, then, the river should have its way.

"Get aboard and take the stern seat," I said to Sah-né-to [Schultz's wife, Natahki, also known as Fine Shield Woman], and as soon as she had done so, I pushed out into the stream. Splash! Sah-né-to dropped a little beaded buckskin sack into the water. What it contained I know not, nor did I ask. But I heard her low prayer: "Spirits of the water, people of the depths, accept my poor sacrifice. Pity us, I entreat you; draw us not down to our death in your cold, dark realm; cast us not upon the rock hidden by the foaming current. Pity, pity. Accept my offering, I pray you, and harm us not."

Sah-né-to has not forgotten the gods and devils of her people if she has been married to a pale-face these twenty

3

years and more. Missionaries and their creeds are as nothing to her; the sun, the glorious, dazzling, resplendent orb, is the kind and living ruler of the world. By his aid, and through sacrifice, the evil spirits may be kept from working harm.

I set the oars and pulled a few long, steady strokes; aided by the swift current we sped downstream at a rate of five miles an hour at least. It seemed only a moment or two since we had cast off, and here we were already at the lower end of the town and opposite the old adobe fort—that is, what is left of it. Of the great thick-walled fortress [Fort Benton] nothing now remains but the southeast bastion, and that, too, would have long since fallen had not a generous and public-spirited one of the old-timers roofed it over, and shored up its crumbling walls. Cannon no longer point from its deep port holes ready to discharge a hail of trade balls into some party of attacking redskins. That day has long since passed. Built in 1856 by the American Fur Company, this fort was for years the center of a vast and far-reaching fur trade. Hundreds of thousands of buffalo robes, like numbers of wolf and beaver skins, and pelts of the deer and elk were brought to it by Indian and white from the far North, from the South, from the Rockies and the vast extent of plains surrounding it, and were later shipped down the river to St. Louis.

Sah-né-to gazed long and sadly at the solitary bastion. "How well I remember," she said, "coming to the great fort with my father and mother to trade. When spring came and the horses had become strong from eating the new green grass, the whole camp came here to trade the winter's take of robes and furs. No matter how great the distance—maybe from the Red Deer River of the North, perhaps from the Yellowstone, or the foothills of the Rockies, or from some point far down the river— here we always came in the early spring. When the men of the fort saw us coming down the hills into the valley, they raised a great flag and fired cannon to greet us. We were many in

4

those days, and when we moved, people on horseback, and horses packed and drawing travois and lodge poles, made a wide, dark streak on the plains miles long. The great chiefs, the proud warriors, rode in the lead when we neared the fort, all dressed in their war costumes. And when the flag was raised and the cannon boomed, they fired their guns and charged up to the gates singing the song of joy and friendship.

"Then the great white chief came out and shook hands with them, and invited them in to feast and smoke, and tell of the experiences of the winter. And while they sat in the room with the great white chief, outfit after outfit came hurrying down the hill, the women shouting and whipping up their horses, lodge poles rattling and clashing, travois jouncing and bouncing as they were hurriedly dragged along. And then one by one and by twos and threes and fives the lodges were put up on the plain near the river, fires were built, and soon hundreds of columns of smoke were rising to join the clouds.

"When the feast and the talk were over the chiefs came home to their lodges, each carrying a present of some kind. My father always brought something away from the white man's table for me and I would watch for him and run to meet him. Sometimes he brought me a hardtack, sometimes a lump of sugar, and taking it from him I would run on ahead to our lodge and show my mother what he had given me. Such little things were highly prized in those days, especially by the children; only once or twice a year did they become the fortunate possessors of a cracker or bit of brown sugar. But no; we were never hungry. Always the lodge was provided with meat; meat of the buffalo, the elk, the deer and antelope; and we had berries, quantities of the various kinds, dried for winter use."

On we went past the fort, and down over the Shonkin bar at the mouth of the stream of that name which puts in here from the Highwood Mountains to the south. It is a stream no longer. Once it was a good-sized creek of pure mountain water. Schools of trout lived in its clear depths, and the beavers bridged it with their dams. Then came the white man and used the water to irrigate vast tracts of the barren plain, so nothing now runs in the old channel but a little seepage of brown alkaline water. The trout are dead, the beavers have vanished, never to return.

A little farther down we passed the "Groscondunez." Here the Teton River makes an elbow to the south at the apex of which it is divided from the Missouri only by a narrow, sharp, high ridge. Along its crest runs an old Indian trail, a short cut from the fort to the mouth of the Marias. It was here, in 1865, that the Piegan chief, Little Dog, met his death, murdered by his own people.

The Piegans then were bitter enemies of the whites. They would come to the fort professing peace and trade their robes, but parties of the warriors were out at all times of the year traveling even as far south as the California Overland Trail in search of scalps and plunder. Of the whole tribe Little Dog alone was the white man's friend, and by every means in his power he tried to keep his people at peace with them, even shooting one or two of the most obstinate and bloodthirsty. He was the especial favorite of the factor of the American Fur Company, Major [Andrew] Dawson, who gave him many valuable presents from time to time, and often sent him down the Missouri on the company's boats that he might see something of the world. His warriors feared him, for he ruled them with an iron hand, and they were jealous of the favors showered on him. No one had such fine guns, such brilliantly colored blankets, such durable saddles and bridles as he.

One day four or five of the more hot-headed warriors held a secret council and determined that, if the tribe was to keep up its record of scalps and plunder taken, their chief must die. The camp was then at the mouth of the Marias, some twelve miles below the fort, and they knew that Little Dog was up there visiting the factor, and would return home that afternoon. So they went up to the Groscondunez and lay in wait for him. At dusk he came riding leisurely along, humming his favorite war song. As one man they leveled their rifles and fired at him, and he fell from his horse without a cry or groan, stone dead.

Strange to relate, every one of his murderers died within a year; some in battle, some by disease, and one by a fall while running buffalo. The people said it was because the sun was angry at their foul deed and had forsaken them. It was an unlucky day for the tribe when their chief was killed. Relieved from the restraint his unbending will had imposed, the braves began a systematic warfare against the whites. Lone trappers and hunters — "woodhawks" — along the river, travelers on the Oregon Trail, and the trail between Fort Benton and the mines to the west were waylaid and murdered by scores and scores. And then came that January morning in '70 when Colonel [E. M.] Baker and his two companies of infantry crept up the edge of the bluff on the Marias overlooking a part of the Piegan camp, some eighty lodges.

There was a massacre! There the whites avenged the death of many an unfortunate pioneer, of many a helpless wife and child. Of all the inmates of those eighty lodges, but three escaped. Men, women and children were indiscriminately shot and then burned in piles of their lodges and household effects. It was a severe lesson, but in no other way could the Piegans have been taught to cease their murderous ways; from that day they took no more white scalps.

Little Dog was Sah-né-to's uncle. No wonder, then, that as we passed the scene of his untimely death, she was for a time somewhat depressed in spirits. But on such a lovely morning no one could long have sad thoughts. The sun shone

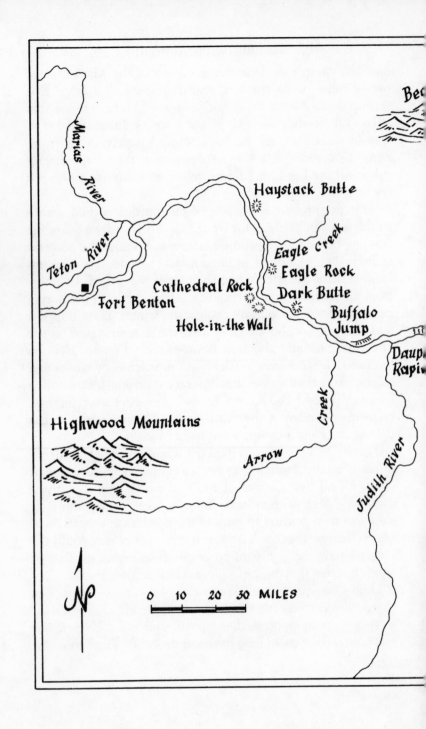

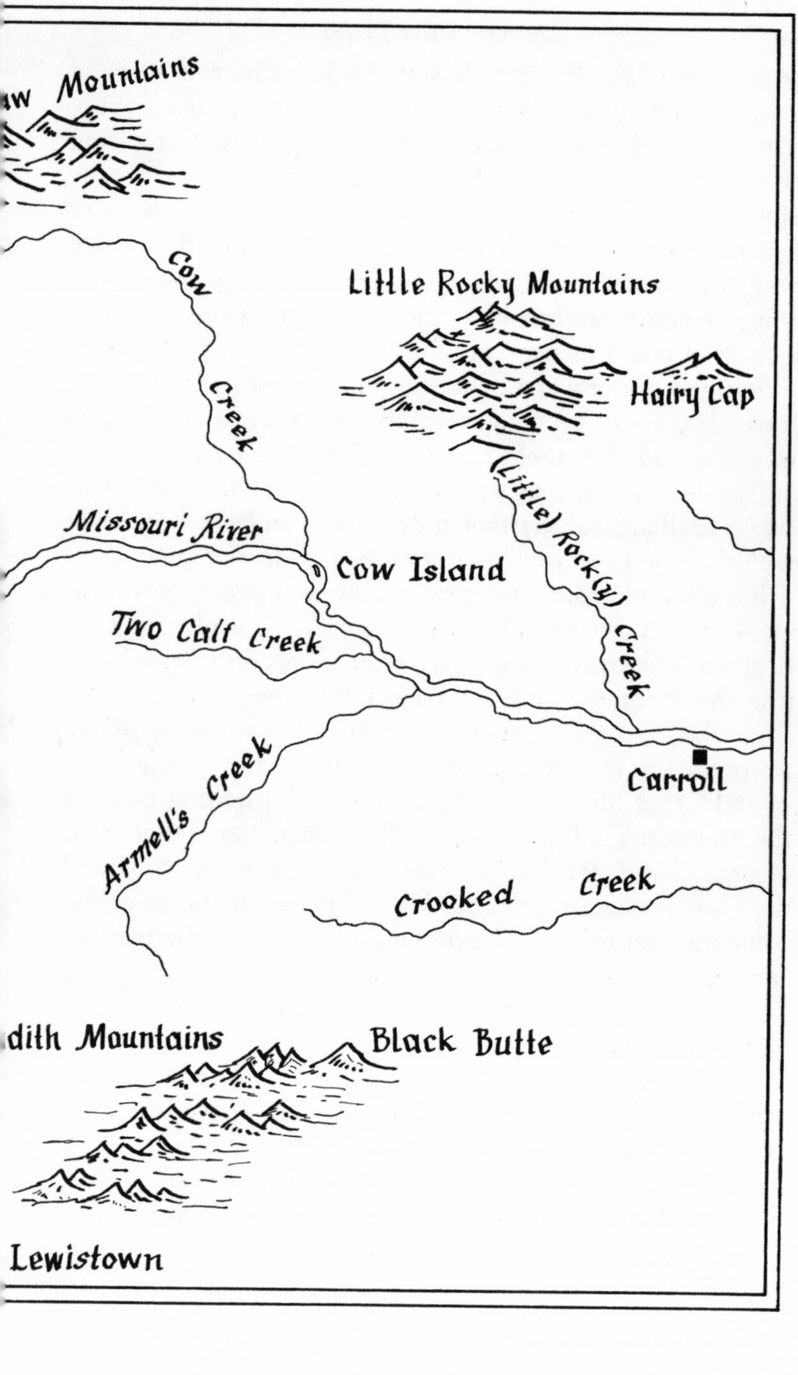
aw Mountains
Cow Creek
Little Rocky Mountains
Hairy Cap
(Little) Rock(y) Creek
Missouri River
Cow Island
Two Calf Creek
Armell's Creek
Carroll
Crooked Creek
dith Mountains
Black Butte
Lewistown

from a clear sky; the river flowed swiftly by narrow strips of timber fringing the shore, yellow and red painted by the early frosts. Here we passed a sheer cut bank reaching from the water's edge up to the level of the plain. On the opposite side there would be a gentle slope of gray sagebrush and buffalo grass. Magpies flew back and forth across the stream with discordant cries. Ducks were a-wing seeking some muddy slough where a rich breakfast might be found. Here and there a flock of chickens were lined up on the shore taking their morning drink of water. The sharptail grouse are interesting birds. Have you ever approached a flock on a cool, frosty morning and seen them running about chasing each other, and all the time keeping up their peculiar and inimitable gabble? The Blackfeet say that they have a language, and talk with each other as well as human beings do.

It was too pleasant a morning to row, and after the sun was an hour high too warm for much exertion; so we let the boat float with the current, dipping a blade now and then to keep it in the channel. It was ten o'clock when we arrived at the Brule Bar, and gliding down over the riffles we went ashore to stretch our legs and gather a few bullberries. It was here, in 1833, that Mr. James Kipp established a trading post for the American Fur Company. It will be remembered that when George Catlin, the Indian artist and philanthropist, visited the Upper Missouri in 1832, Mr. Kipp was in charge of the company's post in the Mandan village, and that the two became great friends. The fort built here did not last long; the Blackfeet finally succeeding in burning it, with all its contents, and murdering a part of its inmates. After some search, we found the site of the fort—just some long, low, grass-grown mounds of dirt and a few fire-cracked rocks where the chimney had stood.

While Sah-né-to was gathering the berries, I flushed a covey of chickens and got three of them with my repeating shotgun

before they could fly out of range. Then we got aboard once
more and continued our journey. At noon we arrived at the
mouth of the Marias River, twenty-two miles from Fort Benton. This is the stream which Lewis and Clark thought was
the main fork of the Missouri, and which they followed up
for some distance until convinced of their mistake. It is a
large stream, draining an immense scope of mountain country, its principal tributaries being the Cutbank, Two Medicine, Badger, Birch and Dupuyer Creeks. All of them rise in
the fastnesses of the Rockies, and are fed by the perpetual
ice and snows of the higher ranges. We landed on a dry, sandy
bar at the mouth of the river and had lunch, washing it down
with long draughts of the cool but slightly muddy water. "It
is the water of the Two Medicine also," said Sah-né-to. "I
wonder when this cupful passed by our ranch up there in the
foothills. Perhaps our son saw these very drops dancing down
over the riffles at the ford."

We rested an hour and then went on. Passing the Spanish
Islands Sah-né-to discovered a flock of green wing teal asleep
on a bar. I stopped rowing and picked up the gun, while she
guided the boat straight toward them. When within thirty
or forty yards of them they began to stretch their necks uneasily and waddle down to the water's edge. There they took
wing, but at the crack of the gun five of them dropped into
the water and were presently picked up.

At four thirty we came in sight of the "Coal Banks," so
named on account of some deposits of inferior lignite in the
bluffs at the lower end of the big bottom. We had made forty-
two miles since daylight. I remembered that on my last trip
down the river in April, 1882, we had camped for the night
in a narrow strip of cottonwood and willows, and thither I
directed Sah-né-to to steer the boat. We found on landing
that we were within the bounds of an accursed sheep ranch;
but in memory of old times I decided to camp there anyhow,

and in a few minutes the tent was up, a fire going in the sheet-iron stove, and preparations for a good dinner under way.

The winter of 1881–82 was the last good season of the buffalo robe trade on the Upper Missouri. I had been employed by Mr. Joseph Kipp [mixed-blood son of James Kipp] for several years at his Carroll trading post. In March of '82 we ran out of whisky, and there were thousands of Crees, Blackfeet and Bloods camped about us. Every lodge had numbers of prime robes to trade, but our stock of drygoods, provisions, red paint and brass jewelry was not what they wanted. "Give us fire water," they said, "and you get the robes." So I went up to Fort Benton overland, built a large flat boat, loaded it with twenty barrels of cheap whisky, and got it down to Carroll as quickly as I could. In less than two weeks after I landed at the port we had the robes, all of them. As I remember it, there wasn't a single fatal quarrel in the camp during that grand spree. It was a sight never to be forgotten, that of several thousand Indians, men and women, drinking, dancing, singing, and cutting all sorts of queer capers. One day some young Crees and Blackfeet did get into dispute over the ownership of a bottle of the precious spirits, and guns and knives were drawn. Then Crowfoot, the chief of the Blackfeet, and Big Bear, chief of the Crees, jumped into the excited circle with rifles cocked. "Whoever fights," said Crowfoot, "be it Cree or Blackfoot, fights us." "Ai," said Big Bear, "he tells our minds. Back to your lodges, foolish youths, and be ashamed of your hot and idle words."

They slunk away at once.

While I sat and mused over those good old times, Sah-né-to had been busy with the dinner, and now she announced that it was ready. Broiled breast of chicken, baked potatoes, hot biscuits, stewed bullberries, a cup of black coffee. I did the meal full justice. Darkness had long since settled down over the valley. The stars came out, the owls began their nightly concert, a coyote ki-yied and yelped on the opposite side of the river. There was nothing to disturb our contentment except the distant bleating of the accursed sheep. And so, after a smoke or two, we went to bed with pleasant anticipations of the wonderful scenery we were to pass through on the morrow.

II

WE were brought back from the land of dreams by the keen whistle and beat of wings. Numerous flocks of water fowl were faring up and down the river — ducks principally, yet not a few gray geese were also passing, and their honking was most pleasant to hear. It was half-past four. I arose and lit the lantern, and then stuffing the stove with cottonwood bark had its top and sides glowing hot in no time. It did not take Sah-né-to long to prepare breakfast. Broiled teal, fried potatoes, hot biscuits and strong, fragrant coffee furnished us an ample and satisfying meal.

We had everything packed and stowed away in the Good Shield at daybreak. There had been a heavy frost during the night, and thin wisps of fog were rising from the water. There was not enough, however, to obscure a glimpse now and then of the channel, so we pushed out into the stream and bent to the oars. From the Coal Banks to the mouth of Little Sandy Creek, about five miles, the course of the river is almost due north; then it turns to the east again. As we were passing the creek Sah-né-to sighted a flock of geese sitting on the lower point of an island opposite it. "Stop rowing," she said. "There are some whitenecks."

But even as she spoke they began to honk and rose from the shore, flying away down the river. Then they turned and came back, mounting higher and higher as they approached. They were probably eighty yards distant when directly over us, but I chanced a shot and was somewhat surprised to see one come tumbling and whirling down and strike the water with a splash that sent it high in fine spray. We held the boat back and waited for the fowl to drift down to us, and then drew it aboard. It was a young one and extremely plump.

15

Five miles below the Little Sandy we came to the first of the remarkable formations which the old river during countless years has gradually exposed to view. Here in the center of a wide level bottom stands the Haystack Butte, round, jagged, of dark volcanic rock and several hundred feet in height. Its sides are perpendicular for a part of the way, and then slope up to a sharp point. It is an odd sight, the lone butte standing there on the level plain. Away to the north of it and across the river to the south the bluffs are of white sandstone and blue clay; no rock of its character being anywhere in sight. As seen from the river, it is doubtful if it could be climbed. The eagles seem to think it a safe place to rear their young and nest upon it every season. As we passed we saw a couple of the birds soaring above it.

Not far below Haystack Butte the valley becomes much narrower. The wide bottoms disappear and from either shore there is a steep ascent to the foot of the bluffs or cliffs. These are of sandstone of varying degrees of density, and in color passing from brown to dazzling white. Some of it is so soft that the rains and melted snow have fluted and carved it with all the precision of a sculptor's chisel. Here and there along these cliffs, sometimes in groups of from dozens to hundreds, and of various heights, stand slender columns of sandstone, capped by circular pieces of a dark and harder variety, giant mushrooms of stone. And again all sorts of fantastic shapes come into view, which my poor pen is utterly unable to describe. With the camera I tried to catch some of the remarkable features of the valley, but the distances were too great. Nothing but canvas and colors, the touch of a great artist, could faithfully portray them.

Along through the canyon, as it may aptly be termed, the river flows very swiftly. In a short time we arrived at the mouth of Eagle Creek, fourteen miles from our starting point in the morning. Just below here stands a thin wall of rock, rising from the water's edge straight up for several hundred feet and running back northward until merged in sandstone bluff. The wall is built up, layer upon layer, of blocks of the stone of unvarying width and thickness, but of different lengths, which, singularly enough, always overlap, so that no interstice is more than the height of the block. On the opposite side of the river the continuation of the wall can be seen, jutting from the southern bluff. How long has it taken the old river to tear the half-mile gap in it?

Sah-né-to said that this great wall was built by Old Man when he made the world. I objected to her theory on the ground that no man could have lifted the massive blocks.

"Just by jumping," she replied, "he made the backbone of the world (the Rockies). Why, then, had he not the power to lift those rocks?"

I answered not. Surely it was no more of a fable than certain others we wot of; the rock, for instance, that gushed water upon the blow of a certain ancient individual's staff.

The river flows by the great wall with a sullen roar, battling with and wearing against some great boulders which impede its course. It is a deceptive stream, this old Missouri, generally so silent in its flowing toward the sea that one would think it had no life. But where a rock or snag impedes its course there is a hissing and roaring and foaming of water which tell of its power and haste. And then on its bosom there is a constant upheaving and sucking swirling which explains only too well the reason why the best of swimmers fear to breast its tide; the undertow seizes them and claims them for its own. The drowning man in this stream does not rise twice or thrice before he finally succumbs. Once drawn beneath the surface his body will only reappear long after death and miles and miles below the scene of the accident, where it may be found cast up on a bar and half-buried in sand. Years ago, one such victim of the river we found, left by the receding waters on a shelving bank, a swollen and shapeless form. We fastened some rocks about its waist with willow withes and consigned it to the depths. Who he was, how he met his fate, we never learned.

For some miles below Eagle Creek there are many narrow walls of the volcanic rock protruding from the clay and sandstone formation, some of them rising from the water's edge. Nearly all of them run due north and south, but in one place a double wall nearly encircles a hill, for all the world like the walls of an ancient city.

Another hour of lazy drifting brought us to Kipp's Rapids, named after that intrepid successor of Lewis and Clark, who established the American Fur Company's post at the mouth of the Marias in 1833. Here on his voyage up the river with his long, deep "keel" boat, he found the water so shallow that he was obliged to make a portage of the cargoes. The water could not have been lower then than it was when we went over the riffles, for we bumped the gravel several times, and the boat drew only eleven inches. I fancied I could see those sturdy cordelliers bending, straining, tugging on the long rope with which they drew their heavily laden boat against the swift current. Here, waist and even neck deep in the cold water, there wading over a bed of quicksand or mud, and again forcing their way through a tangle of willows and prickly rose brush, they toiled early and late. The rough rope chafed sores on their shoulders, which formed into hard calluses and cracked and bled every morning. Their feet were blistered by the water and sand. At night they gathered around the fire and dried their clothes while they ate their simple meal of meat and tea. Then, retreating into the willows or sagebrush away from the decaying flames of the fire, they lay down to sleep, their freshly primed flintlocks by their side, hoping no sneaking war party would disturb them.

But there was a bright side to their life. It was not always a battle against the swift current of the river. There were the happy days in the winter; the excitement of the chase, the pleasant evenings in their warm quarters in the post. And then in the spring the long, delightful sail of three thousand miles down to St. Louis, the meeting with friends and sweethearts, and the grand carouse. What would we dilettanti hunters of today not give to see the valley of the Missouri, teeming with game as it did, countless herds of buffalo, elk and deer; bands of antelope and sheep, droves of wolves and everywhere the grizzlies, singly, in twos and threes and dozens. Oh, theirs was the life!

Just below Kipp's Rapids, on the north side, is a dark cliff jutting out from the river of the valley, named Eagle Rock. At the very top of it Sah-né-to discovered something which she was sure she saw move slightly. I got out the glass and found that it was a lone bighorn, a ram, standing at the verge of the precipice watching us and occasionally stamping with his forefeet. And there he stood until we passed out of sight. Two miles from the rapids we passed Citadel Bluff, also on the north side of the river. It is at least a quarter a mile long, and its summit looks for all the world like the pictures one sees of fortresses of the Middle Ages. One could well imagine it swarming with armored men, bristling with gleaming pikes and spears. We drifted along by with the current enjoying the view of it from different points, and meanwhile I told Sah-né-to of the ancient fortresses it resembled, and of the men of those times who wore shirts of mail, helmets of steel and whose weapons were the bow and arrow, spears and swords.

"How silly they were," she said. "Men cannot fight weighted down with a mass of iron; the battle belongs to the agile and swift of foot."

Rounding a bend we came in sight of Cathedral Rock, a dark upheaval of volcanic rock on the south side, rising straight up from the water to the height of several hundred feet. The side facing the river terminates in a slender spire, and from the base of this the formation runs back toward the bluff, like the roof of a church. We passed close under its ice-scarred wall, the slow eddying and swirling of the water there indicating great depth.

"Surely," said Sah-né-to, "some of the water people must live down there; they love the deep, still places."

Half a mile farther on we came to a thin strip of cottonwood and willow, service and bullberry brush fringing the shore; just back of it there was a narrow, level strip of grass land at the foot of the steep rise of the hills. "Why not camp?" Sah-né-to asked. And nothing loth, although the sun was still an hour high, I pulled in to the shelving bank. We soon had the tent up on the level strip of grass, and everything made snug for the night. Then, taking my rifle I struck up an old game trail, which ran along the comb of a ridge up toward the far-away level of the plain.

It was a deep old trail, sunk far below the level of the ground by the countless feet of buffalo, elk, and deer which had traversed it in years gone by. I was not a little pleased to find that it was still used by the wild creatures of the valley. Here were numerous tracks of the coyote and wolf, and among them the fresh footprints of some mountain sheep — ewes and their young — and the long, tapering impressions of a buck mule deer's hoofs. If I could only get you, old fellow, I thought, how pleased Sah-né-to would be. Ever since leaving home she had been wishing for some *ni-tap-i-wak-sin*, which, in plain English, means real food. Birds and such like she could eat, but meat, real fresh, was what she wanted.

So I sprinted up the steep ridge after that deer, stopping now and then to get my breath and at the same time admire the wonderful view of valley, and winding river, sculptured cliffs and pinnacles spread out on either hand. Up and up, past deep cut barren coulees, past clumps of juniper and groves of stunted pine, and ever the tracks of the big buck were before me, enticing me on into the sunset and descending shades of the night. At last I was obliged to turn back, for the waning light no longer afforded a clear view of the rifle sights. How I ran down that ridge. The ground was soft, and jump as I would, I felt no jar. It seemed but a few moments until I came in sight of the tent, glowing like a pale opal from the light within. And then I caught the appetizing odor of fried chicken, coffee and other good things.

As I sat down on the edge of our couch, Indian fashion, and the good cook set them before me, I thanked my stars that yet, even in this late day, there was a place left where one could get away from the discordant sounds of civilization — even the lowing of cattle — where nature had ever reigned supreme. And then, after the satisfying smoke, we lay down on the restful couch and went to sleep, serenaded by the coyotes and wolves far up in the breaks. Long may they escape the deadly poisons and traps of men.

Again we were afloat at daybreak. A warm west wind had blown during the night, and there was no fog. When the sun arose above the horizon, gilding the white bluffs and time-worn sandstones of the valley's rim, we thought we had never beheld a fairer or more weird piece of nature's handiwork. Sah-né-to was moved to tears. I know not what was her simple prayer to the rising king of day — yes, I know; but why repeat her earnest supplications to her god? Who knows but what they were of as much avail as those of the Christian to his unseen God?

The Hole in the Wall! Never a traveler on the Upper Missouri but remembers that wonderfully thin, high wall of sandstone. From the top of a high ridge it juts straight out over the valley and then drops straight down, hundreds of feet, to the level of the plain. Some fifty feet back from its fall, and perhaps twenty from its crest, some blocks of the stone have dropped out, leaving an oblong, jagged hole. When we came in sight of it, for a moment the sun shone through it, illuminating a bit of hill and river with an intense light, and leaving all the rest of the valley in dark shadows. No travelers were more careful to record the physical aspect of the country they passed through, than were Lewis and Clark, yet I find no mention of this remarkable freak of nature in their journal. Perhaps in their time it was a solid wall.

There were numerous flocks of Canada geese along the river this morning. From every bar and island point they arose ahead of us with a din of honks that echoed from bluff to bluff in the still morning air. I had many opportunities to go ashore and creep upon them, sheltered by high banks and growth of willow, but we had one fat one in the boat, and that was sufficient for our needs. For an hour or more after starting, we saw many flocks of chickens—sharptails, of course —coming to the river's edge for their morning drink. Once there were a number of them running about among a flock of geese, the two species apparently paying no attention to each other. As a rule, the chickens came to water but once a day at this season, spending the rest of the day far back at the heads of the coulees. Earlier, in August, September and October, while the weather is warm, they can always be found near the river. I would not dare to estimate the number of those birds on the upper river from the Coal Banks, say, to old Fort Peck. Along this stretch of nearly three hundred miles by water, they have never been disturbed, and are as plentiful as they were a hundred, or, for that matter, a thousand years ago.

From Cathedral Rock the river runs northeast for five miles, and then turns sharply to the southeast. Rounding the bend, we found a moderate breeze blowing in our favor, so I pulled in the oars and hoisted a small, square sail of muslin I had brought for just such an occasion. Aided by the current, we sped rapidly along through a continuation of the wonderful scenery of the day before. Here were the Pinnacles, a succession of needle points of sandstone, varying from a foot to fifty in height. And then we came to Steamboat Rock, a high, long, massive butte lying a mile north of the river. I never could see its resemblance to a steamer. On both sides of it and beyond, far to the north, are a succession of odd-shaped buttes and hills typical of this weird country.

In another hour we came to the Dark Butte, a sharp, high mass of brown conglomerate, pumice and clay, rising from the river's edge to a height of at least five hundred feet. Passing here on the steamer *Red Cloud* in 1880 we espied a big mountain ram almost at its summit, curiously looking down at the boat. One of our party, Eli Guardipee, knelt down on the deck, and resting his rifle on the rail, took a careful aim at the animal before he fired. At the report of the gun the ram made one bound straight up in the air, fell on its side and then rolling, tumbling, sliding, splashed into the river. The steamer was stopped at once and the great stern wheel held it back until the ram floated alongside, when the deck hands drew it aboard. That was a splendid and difficult shot, as the boat was making at least twenty miles an hour. If almost any other man had made it, I would have thought it a scratch, but Eli—well, more of him and his marksmanship later.

Down past the Dark Butte and around a bend we came to Pablos Island, named after an old employee of the American Fur Company. The upper part of it is a long, wide sand bar, but the lower end has a fine growth of tall, slender cottonwoods. Just below it are Pablos Rapids. As we came into them I was so absorbed in the scenery to the north that I forgot to point out the channel to Sah-né-to, and with a rude bump the Good Shield ran hard aground. I put on my waders and finally got her out into deeper water, although it was hard work against the swift current. From the rapids we had a run of fast water to Wolf Island, why and when so named I never learned. And then a couple of miles farther on we came to the mouth of Arrow Creek and landed for lunch, having made sixteen miles since daybreak.

Arrow Creek rises in the Highwood Mountains, and for part of its course flows through a deep and narrow valley, in places a walled canyon. At its confluence with the Missouri it has formed a wide and beautiful plain, ever pushing the old river further and further northward against the hills. There is a beautiful grove of timber along the edge of the plain skirting the river. Just back of it we found the ruins of an old woodhawk's and hunter's home, half-cabin and half-dugout. Nothing was standing except the fireplace and chimney of uncut rock. At one side of it was a great heap of bones, skulls, and horns of the buffalo, elk, deer and mountain sheep. It was not all work for the old-time woodhawks, the men who supplied the steamers with fuel. Betimes they hunted and trapped, and took life easy. Many a pleasant evening they spent in front of the old fireplace after a long day's work or tramp. Many a tale of adventure they told as they watched a great side of fat ribs brown and crisp before the glowing coals.

After lunch Sah-né-to remarked with rather an appealing look, I thought, that she had found some heavily laden brushes of bullberries back in the brush. "And you want to gather them?" I asked. "Very well, then, we will camp. We will take our time on this trip, even if we get frozen in somewhere below."

III

AFTER putting up the tent and getting camp in shape, I shouldered my rifle and started up the valley. There is a thin fringe of cottonwood and willow bordering the creek and for a time I tramped along the edge of it looking for signs of game. Water was standing in pools here and there in the creek bed. The ranchers away up in the Judith Basin have long since diverted Arrow Creek to irrigate their homesteads, and it is no longer a running stream except during the June rains. Every one of the pools I came to was covered with ducks, mallards, widgeons, and teal. From the rose and buck brush sharptail grouse were constantly rising ahead of me and lighting again after a flight of two or three hundred yards. And then, suddenly, a lone whitetail buck bounded out of a little grove of cottonwoods and made for the hills as fast as he could run.

I fired at him twice, and was about to pull the trigger a third time, when he made a last leap and fell dead into the bottom of a coulee. I did not cut his throat, for by the location of the bullet hole I knew that he had bled internally, and upon opening him found that I was right. Sah-né-to had heard my shots and joined me, and how pleased she was at my success. I cut off the buck's head, first taking the tongue, and then, shouldering the carcass, we returned to camp. It was not a large deer, only a three-year-old, but it got very heavy, and I had to rest often before we arrived at the tent. There was a convenient tree in front of it, and running a stick through the deer's gambrels I hoisted it up to the nearest limb, clear of the ground.

A hunter never feels just right until he has hung up a piece of meat in camp. There may be ducks, and chickens, and geese galore strung around, but the feeling of absolute contentment never comes until a deer or an elk, a sheep or an antelope, sways to the breeze from a nearby limb. So, at least, I felt, and Sah-né-to too; we had the "real food," *ni-tap-i-waksin,* she had been longing for. And then, I felt rather proud of having killed the deer; for nineteen years I had not fired at a running animal, and yet I had dropped this one in two shots. Perhaps I owed my success to the Lyman sights. I had never before used them, but subsequent experience leads me to believe that it is nearly as difficult to miss as to kill with them.

Dinner was over, the dishes washed, a quantity of dry wood piled behind the stove. Sah-né-to lit the lantern and resumed work on a pair of moccasins she was embroidering with a vine-like pattern of various colored cut beads. "Tell me," I said, "why this stream is named Ap-si-sak-ta—the Arrow River?"

"It was given that name long ago," she replied, "by the ancient ones, on account of a strange, a very strange, thing which took place. One time in that long ago there was a beautiful young girl named Ah-we-kas—the Antelope—the daughter of a chief. She was as good as she was handsome, and very industrious. No one tanned whiter buckskin, softer robes than she. No wonder, then, that all the young men were her slaves, and longed to make her their wife. But to all of them she replied, 'No,' and remained with her parents, doing all she could for their welfare and happiness. One after another the great men, the rich men of the camp, made offers to the old people for her, offers of horses and other wealth, but always her parents would ask her if she was willing, and when she replied, 'Nay,' they did not urge her. So the girl grew up, year by year more and more beautiful, and reached womanhood. 'Tis said that her hair when unbraided almost swept the ground; that her large, soft eyes were like those of

26

a fawn, deep and clear, with an expression in them—I cannot say just what—that made the heart of man beat furiously in his bosom. She was tall and slender, yet of a rounded and graceful figure. She could run like a deer, and swim with the speed of an otter.

"One spring the people were camping for a time somewhere on this river. One day there came from the camp of the Blackfeet, far to the north, a young man to visit his Piegan relatives, and that very evening he was invited by the father of Ah-we-kas to come to his lodge and feast. The young woman set some food before him, took one look at his face and hurriedly returned to her seat. He had one glimpse into her lovely eyes and was so distraught that he could not eat. In that one glance both knew that they were made for each other. After that the young Blackfoot came to her lodge every day and talked long with her father of the north country, of the doings of his people—of their wars, their hunts and adventures. But he never spoke to her, nor she to him; but if they gazed at one another shyly, bashfully, as lovers will—well, what harm?

"At last, one day, the young man informed the chief that on the morrow he would return to his people, 'But,' he continued, 'I shall soon return, driving many horses before me.'

"As he passed out of the lodge somehow his hand met that of the girl, and he gave it a gentle squeeze; she in turn pressed his, and then covered her head with her robe in shame of her boldness.

"'I wonder, now,' the old man mused, 'what he meant by that—that he would soon return driving many horses before him?'

"Ah-we-kas was sure she knew, but made no reply.

"Most importunate of all her suitors was Black Bull, a man of savage temper and a great warrior. He was tall, and broad, and heavy, of great strength, and as homely as he was strong.

By his success in war he had become very rich; no one owned more horses, no one had a greater store of weapons, fine garments, robes and furs, than he. Two wives he had already, women whom he forced to toil incessantly, and whom he cruelly beat when anything went wrong. And now he wanted Ah-we-kas for his third wife. Almost daily he sent word to her father, offering this and that for her, until finally the messenger carried this: 'Thus says the Black Bull: Take my whole herd and of the rest of my property what you will, and give me your daughter in return.'

"But, as before, the answer went back: 'No, she refuses you.'

"Then Black Bull became angry, beat his wives, and rushed madly out of his lodge and away he knew not where. Passing the trail to the river he met Ah-we-kas and raised his hand to strike her, a fearful scowl on his face. Then he changed his mind and cried out: 'And so you refuse me; know, then, that you shall yet become my wife, or die.'

"'Twas but a few days after this that the young Blackfoot returned, driving before him, as he had said he would, a band of fine horses, red and white, yellow and white, black and white; all of them spotted horses. And his relatives took the horses and tied them up about the lodge of the father of Ah-we-kas, and gave him the young man's message.

"'What say you now?' the old man asked his daughter. 'What word have you for this new suitor?'

"Burning with shame, her head bent low, she pressed his wrinkled hand and whispered: 'You may keep the horses.'

"So they were married. When Black Bull heard the news he cursed them and his unpropitious gods, and swore to have revenge. A day or two later Ah-we-kas went to the river for water, and as she stooped down at the shore Black Bull sprung upon her, bore her to the ground, and lifted his knife to stab her in the side. But even as the blow was descending the knife dropped from his hand, and with a groan he fell quivering on her senseless form, an arrow buried in his back. And there he died. The girl, recovering from her faint, shrieked long and loud, and people came running to her aid. They drew the dead man away, and noticing the arrow sticking in his back, withdrew it. No one had seen its like before; the polished shaft was black and heavy, the tip was long and broad, and made of some white substance neither bone nor stone, but most resembling bone; the feathers, stiff and well wrapped on were from some unknown bird, and had all the colors of the rainbow. The warriors looked long and curiously at it as 'twas passed from hand to hand, and then bethought them to search for the one who had owned and shot it. But Mik-sik-um, wisest of medicine men, stopped them. 'Search not,' he cried, 'for 'twill be of no avail; the owner of this arrow is not visible to mortal eyes. This man lies dead, the victim of his own bad heart and passions. 'Tis a judgment of the gods. Let his women bury him at once and get him from our sight.'

"And so," Sah-né-to concluded, "this river got its name."

"And the arrow?" I asked. "Whence came it? Who shot it?"

"How stupid you are," she replied. "For her goodness and virtue Ah-we-kas was favored by the sun. In her time of need he aided her. He shot the arrow, of course. Mik-sik-um, the medicine man, knew that as soon as he saw it, for he was wise in the mysteries of his craft."

"Well, anyhow, Sah-né-to," I said, "'tis a good story, and we will not question the truth of it. Put another stick in the stove for the night is chilly."

I lit a smoke and after a little continued: "But, say, Sah-né-to, don't you think the young Blackfoot might have shot that arrow? It was of strange material and make, but he might have obtained it from some far northern tribe, people whom the Piegans had never heard of."

"No."

"Why?"

"Because."

I had no more to say, and smoked in silence. When a woman says "because," a man is up against it.

Somehow we were a little late in loading up the next morning and resuming our voyage. I didn't regret it, however, as I wanted to examine a place a mile or two farther down the river where Lewis and Clark had found the remains of one hundred and twenty-six head of buffalo, the animals having been decoyed over a cut bluff by Indians.* From this find they had named Arrow Creek "Slaughter River." But the name did not stick; the voyageurs who followed them, Joseph Kipp and others, learning the Indian name for it, continued to call it as they did, Arrow River or Arrow Creek.

We had no difficulty in locating the scene of the "slaughter." A long level but narrow ridge runs southward from the edge of the valley to the water's edge, where it ends abruptly with a perpendicular drop of more than a hundred feet. In Lewis and Clark's time there was quite a bit of shore between it and the river, but year by year the channel has shifted further and further to the north, and not only the shore but some of the bluff has been eaten away by the current. Landing just below the bluff, I climbed up to the top of it, expecting to find rows of stone piles which generally mark one of these

---

*On Wednesday, May 29, 1805, Captain Meriwether Lewis reported, "today we passed on Stard. side the remains of a vast many mangled carcases of Buffalow which had been driven over a precipice of 120 feet by the Indians and perished; the water appeared to have washed away a part of this immence pile of slaughter and still their remained the fragments of at least a hundred carcases they created a most horrid stench. in this manner the Indians of the Missouri distroy vast herds of buffaloe at a stroke." *Original Journals of the Lewis and Clark Expedition, 1804–1806*, ed., Reuben Gold Thwaites (New York, 1904–1905), II, 93.

"buffalo pounds," as the old voyageurs termed them. There were none on it; if I had had time to walk back to where the ridge left the rim of the valley, I might have found them extending in V form out on the plain. My climb was not without regard, however, for on the way back to the boat I found an obsidian arrowhead. It was a very small and thin one, and precisely like those which are found about an old "buffalo pound" on the Two Medicine River, near the foot of the Rocky Mountains.

From Arrow Creek the river flows nearly due east for five miles. On the south side the hills rise abruptly from the shore; on the north side are three small sagebrush flats. Scattering pines grow in the breaks on either hand. Looking eastward down this stretch we could see in the distance the breaks of the Judith River, dark with their heavy growth of pine and fir.

In due time, turning the bend to the north, we came in sight of a wide gap in the north side of the valley, a flat four or five miles long through which Sage Creek flows into the river. Here we entered Drowned Man's Rapids. That is an ominous name, but they are really the safest rapids in the river. The channel is very narrow here, choked in by hills on either side, and the water rushing through has great depth. Both shores are strewn with huge boulders, and there must be many of them lying down on the bottom judging from the leaping and swirling of the rushing water. We went over the long swells all too quickly to suit the oarsman, who was glad to rest a bit, but it must be confessed that the one who held the rudder gave a sigh of relief when we finally glided into still water. A mile below the rapids we passed the point of a bare ridge on the right, and came in sight of the wide, long flats of the Judith River, opposite those of Sage Creek. I had been told to look for a certain grave in this flat, and re-mark it if necessary.

Below the point of the ridge, at the western edge of the first coulee, and two hundred yards from the river, was the place. We landed at the mouth of the coulee and looked long and carefully for the wooden cross which had marked it, but could not find even a grass-grown mound. Time and the constant wash from the hills had obliterated all traces of it. So all trace of the last resting place of Nathaniel Crabtree, one of the bravest and most careless of men, is lost. It was here he met his fate. He and George Croff had long been partners in the woodyard business, in trapping, hunting and trading.

"In 1865," George told me, just before I left home for this trip, "we had a woodyard at the Coal Banks. Winter and summer buffalo were always in sight of our cabin, but just for a change and a little sport we used to go out to the Bear Paw Mountains once in a while and kill a wagonload of elk, deer, sheep, antelope and bear, using the fat of the latter in lieu of lard. The Indians were always prowling around in those days in search of the white man's scalp and horses, and one never knew when a war party might jump him. So on these hunts, after supper was over, we used to go some distance from the fire and make our beds in a dark piece of woods or brush. On such occasions I would always ask Nat where he had placed his rifle, and nine times out of ten he would reply: 'Oh, I don't know; it's lying somewhere over there by the fire.'

"Well, I'd lecture him about his carelessness, but he always laughed and declared there was no danger, and I usually had to hunt the weapon up and lay it by his side. He was as good a friend and comrade as a man could wish for, honest, brave, good natured, a tireless worker. But he was careless; your good-natured, easy-going men generally are careless.

"In the fall of '67 we moved down to the mouth of the Judith and started to get out wood for the steamboats there, having cut and sold all there was in the vicinity of the Coal

Banks. We built a good-sized cabin on the flat about two miles west of the creek's junction with the Missouri. Camp Cook, a temporary post of three or four companies of mounted infantry, was located on this stream, and some four miles from us, so we felt pretty secure from Indian raids. Still, they used to bother us some, and the soldiers, too. One night a guard saw what he took to be an Indian sneaking up to the tarpaulin-covered supplies he was watching, and called out 'Halt!' a number of times. But the Indian never stopped, and when he got up as close as he wanted to, he leveled his old fuke and gave the soldier a mortal wound. Of course, the whole camp rushed out then, and what do you suppose the officers did? They ordered their men to light a lot of lanterns and search the timber and brush for the Indians! They were a pretty green outfit, both officers and men.

"We had six men in our employ cutting pine up in the breaks and in the hills, but one of them was always on the lookout for any sneaking war party, while the rest worked. Nat and I hauled the wood to the river with three yokes of bulls (oxen). We had no horses, and we took turns going after the cattle in the morning. On the 5th of April, '68, I remember the date well, it was Nat's turn. I got up before daylight to prepare breakfast, and soon afterward he started out, leaving his rifle, as usual. I never went away from the cabin without mine.

"Well, daylight came, and at sunup we had breakfast, but Nat did not return. The men shouldered their axes and rifles and were just starting to their work when we saw the soldiers' herd of horses, some four or five hundred head, running up the long, sloping hill on the west side of the valley of the Judith. And behind them, whooping, yelling and lashing, rode a lot of Indians, urging them on. I felt at once that something had happened to Nat, and we started out to look for him. After going half a mile out on the flat I saw the bulls and turned toward them, and when near the coulee they were feeding in I saw my partner rise up out of the sagebrush, stagger a few steps toward the cabin, and then fall. I hurried to where he had disappeared and found him lying face down in the brush, three arrows sticking in his back. He had fainted. I called the men, and sending one of them for the doctor at Camp Cook, had the rest help me get Nat to the cabin.

"I pulled out two of the arrows, but the third one, which had struck him in the lower part of the back, and was pressing against the lower part of the abdomen, I dared not touch. In a little while Nat recovered from his faint, and after drinking a glass of whisky and water, seemed his old cheerful self again. He had found the bulls, he said, and was going around behind them to drive them in, when five Indians rose up out of the sagebrush only a few yards behind him and fired five arrows into his back. He got hold of the upper ones and pulled them out, and then looked around for a club or a rock with which to defend himself. But there was nothing of the kind in sight, and then the pain became so acute that he grew dizzy, reeled and fell. The Indians started off toward the hills, but after going a short distance one of them turned back, drawing his knife, evidently with the intention of taking his scalp. But Nat's hat had fallen off, exposing his partially bald head, and when the Indian saw the fringe of thin locks he turned and hurried to rejoin his companions.

"The doctor came after a while and extracted the remaining arrow. 'Poor fellow,' he said, 'I fear you're done for,' and leaving a little medicine of some kind to ease the pain, he went away.

"'Of course I'm done for,' Nat told me. 'I knew that as soon as I was shot. But cheer up, old boy, and don't take it so hard; it can't be helped, and we've just got to make the best of it. Yes, I know I ought to have taken my rifle; if I had they would never have molested me. Well, old pard, give me your hand

and let me go to sleep; if I never wake, good-bye and good luck.'

"Those were the last words he ever spoke. He dozed away into a deep sleep, from that into a stupor, quietly breathed his last soon after midnight, and I lost the best friend I ever had. I felt so badly about it that I couldn't bear to stay there any longer, and leaving everything in charge of one of the men, took the first boat for Fort Benton."

Reluctantly giving up our search for the grave, we returned to the boat, and in fifteen or twenty minutes came to the mouth of the Judith, where our friend, Wm. Norris, has a large ranch, ferry and general store. We had not met since the buffalo days, and of course began to talk of old times at once. Norris waters several hundred acres of land back from the river with a ditch from the Judith, and some immense stacks of alfalfa showed what irrigation will do in this dry region. Beside hay, he has succeeded every year in raising field corn, tomatoes, tobacco, melons and sweet potatoes, to say nothing of the commoner vegetables. Looking over the place and talking of other days, the time passed all too quickly, and 'twas sundown before we knew it; so leaving the Good Shield tied to the ferryboat, we camped where we were, and were well cared for.

Lewis and Clark named this stream the Judith, after some Virginia girl they knew. The Blackfeet call it O-to-kwi-tuk-tai — Yellow River, on account of the quantities of yellow "paint" or ochre which is found near its source. The large flat here at its mouth and the Sage Creek flat opposite, were favorite camping places with them, good trails leading out to the plains north and south, and the wide flats affording ample room to graze their herds in sight of their lodges. It was here that the [Governor Isaac I.] "Stevens" treaty of 1855 took place between the Government and the Blackfeet, Crows and Assiniboines. Stevens brought with him a steamboat load of presents for the red men; among other things sacks of coffee, beans, rice and bacon. The Indians prized the sacks, but they had no use for their contents, so they dumped the food out on the ground and went on their way rejoicing.

It is over this treaty that the Indians have since been so angry, especially since the disappearance of the buffalo. They claim that they merely gave the white men permission to make roads and travel through their country, and that the vast territory lying between the Missouri and Yellowstone Rivers still belongs to them. They certainly have a good claim to it; where is the lawyer who will take their case upon a conditional fee?

IV

OUR friend Norris had said that the prairie chickens were not nearly so numerous as they had been the previous season. In the spring great numbers of them had nested in his hay fields, and their nests and young had been destroyed by irrigation. When I stepped out shortly after sunrise, I wondered what the number of the birds could have been the year before, for here they were on every hand in the haystacks, the barn roof, in the trees around, and covey after covey was in the air. Large flocks of ducks were also on the wing, flying up and down the course of the Judith, and geese were honking here and there from their roosts in the sandbars of the river. This was surely an ideal place for sport with gun and dog.

After an early breakfast we boarded the Good Shield and resumed our voyage. A mile below Norris' place we passed a ranch on the opposite side of the river, which depended upon a wheel for irrigation. It was an immense affair of wood and steel rods, sixty feet in diameter, and revolving by the force of the current against its broad blades. Large, deep troughs, or buckets, took up the water and poured it into a long flume extending to the irrigated land. It kept up a constant stream of more than one hundred inches, and that quantity will water a very large acreage.

Passing Council Island, so named from the Council or Treaty of 1855, we shot through the rapids and entered the country Lewis and Clark named the Dark Hills, the highest elevations on the whole course of the river below Great Falls. The formation is brown clay and decomposed pumice stone, in places wholly devoid of verdure. Some of these buttes have sharp summits, others are table-topped and support a crown of pine and fir. In places they rise abruptly from the river's edge, and again there are wide sagebrush flats at their base. There is no place along the river where the sagebrush grows so luxuriantly as in these flats. We startled a couple of mule deer which were browsing along the shore, and they were lost to view as soon as they entered its shelter. But in any case they were safe, as we still had a portion of the buck we had killed at Arrow Creek. The larger part of it had found its way into the larder of our Judith friends, and right glad we were to dispose of it, as we then had an excuse to kill another one in the near future.

The swiftest part of the navigable Missouri is a twenty-six mile stretch east from the Judith; the water is all swift, and there are thirteen rapids in the course. We found well-defined channels of deep water through the Birch, Holmes, McKeevers, Gallatin, Bear and Little Dog rapids, and then drew near the Dauphin Rapids, which I had been worrying about ever since our start from Fort Benton. Years before the Government engineers had run a long wing dam out from the south shore at this point, throwing all the water into one narrow, deep channel. But the ice had battered it season after season, wearing it away, and as I looked now I could see only a line of white foam where it had once stood. The roar of the water was sullen and menacing. On the flat nearby some men were building a cabin, and rowing ashore I walked over to them. "Are you building a sheep ranch?" I asked.

"Not on your life!" one of them replied. "We've got a little bunch of cattle; the sheep men run us out where we were located over on the railroad, and we've found a good range here. The first blankety-blank sheep man that shows up in this vicinity with his flocks had better come heeled, for we'll sure fight."

I sympathized with them. The sheep men are, without doubt, "killing the golden goose"; the luxuriant range which would have lasted forever if stocked with cattle only, is being rapidly ruined by them. And then, what will our children do? There is no great West for them to explore and exploit.

The cattlemen were very sociable. They pointed to a cellar they had dug, about five feet in depth, and said that at the bottom of it their shovels had uncovered the remains of a fire, some .44-caliber cartridge shells and some human bones. There were no cartridges of that kind used in this country until 1866, so in thirty-five years or less the wash from the hills had deposited five feet of soil upon the bottom. How I wished I could know the tragedy which had here taken place. Most likely the bones were the remains of some white men, surprised and murdered by Indians.

Game, especially mule deer, the cattlemen said, was fairly abundant. The day before one of them had seen two good-sized bunches of mountain sheep back in the hills. "But," he continued, with a sly wink, "of course I didn't shoot at them, as the game law prohibits the killing of them at any season of the year."

I asked about the rapids, and was informed that the main channel was full of boulders, two boats having been wrecked on them that season. This was not encouraging, so I decided to investigate a gap I had seen in the wing dam near the south shore. Crossing over, I put on the waders, and staff in hand, ventured out step by step to the center of the opening, finding eighteen inches of water in the shallowest place. Below the gap that part of the stream narrowed considerably, and while it was too swift to be sounded afoot, it looked to have plenty of depth, so I waded back to the boat and determined to try it. We started slowly, with just enough speed to afford steering way. Sah-né-to was frightened and confused by the leaping, foaming, roaring water off to the left, so I bade her let go of the tiller, and steered with the oars. We glided over the shallow place and through the gap without a bump or scrape, and then into the narrow channel; here I could not touch bottom with oars, and felt sure I had solved the problem of the dreaded rapids. And so I had, for in a minute or two we ran safely into the main channel at the foot of them.

I have been unable to learn much about "old man" Dauphin, for whom these rapids were named. He was a French Creole, born in St. Charles, Missouri, and was long an employee of the American Fur Company. In 1857 he resigned from their service and became a "freeman," or free trapper. Employees were known as "company men." In the winter of 1857–58, Dauphin made his headquarters at the mouth of Milk River, trapping for some distance up that stream and on the Missouri. When spring came he made four large, long dugouts, lashed them together, and then piling his beaver skins on them drifted down to St. Louis with the current, nineteen hundred and fifty miles by the channel of the river. What a large number of the flat-tails he must have had.

Below these rapids the hills are lower, the valley wider, the pine groves on the slopes more frequent. Five miles farther down we passed a rock chimney, sole remnant of a once-comfortable woodhawk's cabin. I remembered taking refuge in it once, on a trip up the river on the ice. It was bitterly cold, night was coming on, the horses were tired, and we were looking for a sheltered place to camp when we sighted the cabin. No one was at home, but the latch string hung out, and we took possession of it after unharnessing the horses and picketing them. My half-blood companion built a roaring fire in the broad fireplace and we had some meat roasting, the coffee pot boiling, in short order. Many and many a time since I have thought of the unique chair which stood in front of the hearth. The framework was of large pine poles, over which had been stretched a green buffalo hide, dark and glossy, and heavy furred, the head, where the hair was longest and thickest, forming the seat, the rest of it the long, sloping back. Used day after day as the hide dried, it had shrunk here and given away there, until when it finally set, it fitted every curve of one's body. It was the most comfortable chair I ever sat in, and I determined to make one like it as soon as I got back to our trading post. But one thing or another always prevented, and at last the buffalo were exterminated, and then there was no more of the required material to be had.

The Lone Pine Rapids were met; by the time we came to them a fierce, hot, gusty wind was roaring down the valley and tossing the water so, that I could not make out the channel. However, from the lay of the shore we thought the deep water was next the north side, and chanced it, running through without touching bottom. Then we came in sight of Castle Bluff, a bold, high, white sandstone promontory on the south side of the river. On its rim are all sorts of fantastic carvings of the soft stone by Mother Nature and Father Time, turrets, escarpments and bastions, all capped by the usual portion of dark, hard stone. The bluff was well named. Opposite it are Castle Bluff Rapids, and below them a short distance the Magpie Rapids, through both of which the channel is next to the north shore. We went through them with water to spare, then through a nameless piece of swift water, and finally came to the head of the last one, the Bird Rapids. Just above them on the south side there is a fine grove of cottonwoods, and as the wind was blowing unpleasantly hard, bringing with it occasional squalls of rain, we decided to camp in their shelter.

We tied up, and digging a trail to the top of the bank with a pickax, set out to find a clear place among the willows and buck brush for the tent. Not twenty yards from the shore five whitetail deer broke cover and ran for the hills, on their way starting four more, which ran up the valley. There was no grassy place in the timber, and upon coming to its outer edge we saw something which made us think that we did not care to camp there after all. In the center of the wide flat just above was a deserted woodhawk's cabin, windowless and doorless, and in front of it stood two men watching the deer which had run up that way. Then they turned and looked in our direction long and carefully. With my glass I could see that their faces were covered with beard and that beside their rifles, they each had two revolvers at their belts.

Before leaving Fort Benton I had heard that a certain desperado named Larson, who had escaped from the Canadian mounted police and from the Montana authorities, was in hiding somewhere on the river. At the Judith it was claimed that he had been seen near Cow Island. Also, it was surmised that the Kid Curry gang, murderers and robbers of the Great Northern express car, were still hiding somewhere in these badlands.

Now Sah-né-to knew nothing of this, as she does not understand English, and I had thought best to say nothing about it; but as soon as she saw the men near the deserted cabin, their horses picketed nearby, her suspicions were aroused. "Surely," she said, "these men are not of good heart; let us go on."

And we went. They saw us and hurried toward their horses; we rushed to the boat and pulled across to the north side, where the channel is, and shot down through the rapids. Just below them, at the bend, cut coulees and a high bluff precluded any possibility of their following us horseback if they felt so inclined, but we saw no more of them. Likely they had been badly scared. I hoisted a part of the sail and we fairly flew for about four miles before the fierce wind, landing finally on Sturgeon Island for the night. Its broad, sandy shore was dotted with tracks, fresh and old, of both whitetail and mule deer, and when we came to put up our tent in the shelter of a few cottonwoods, we found their trails and beds everywhere in the tall grass. While unloading the boat two

men passed us in a long, narrow scow. They had up an immense square sail and the craft went with the speed of a steam
launch, piling up a roll of foaming water at the bow. In answer to my hail they shouted that they were from Fort Benton, and bound for "St. Louis or bust." They were undoubtedly frozen in somewhere in the Dacotahs [Dakotas].

Beside deer sign, we had noticed many wolf tracks along
the shore of the island, and shortly after dark, as we sat down
to dinner, a band of the animals serenaded us from the nearby hills. The wind had ceased and their long and melancholy
wails filled the silent valley with vibrant sound. It was pleasant to hear, bringing back many memories to both of us of
other days we had spent along the river and upon the ad-
jacent plains.

Sah-né-to had lost her bearings during our devious wind-
ings through the dark hills. I explained that we were a short
run above the mouth of Cow Creek, the Middle Creek of her
people, so named because it flows through the center of the
gap between the Bear Paw and Wolf Mountains (Little Rockies), on its way southward to the Missouri.

Mention of the creek reminded her of many incidents of
her childhood in this locality. She told of the immense herds
of buffalo which once covered the nearby plains; of the numberless bands of elk and deer and antelope along the foothills of the mountains and the valleys. "How many years ago
was it," she asked, "that Big-Eared White Man (an old trader
named Upham) traveled with us and kept the camp supplied
with cartridges, tobacco and sugar?"

I thought a little and replied that it was exactly twenty-four.

"That was the winter," she said, "we lost my cousin, Weasel
Moccasin, bravest, kindest, most generous of men. We had
camped at the lower south end of the Bear Paws for a long
time, and the daily hunting had finally driven the game away
for some distance in every direction. So one morning my

cousin announced that he would go eastward to the Wolf Mountains for a few days' hunt. A number joined him with wives, taking a few lodges and many pack and travois horses with which to bring back the meat and hides. The next afternoon they came to the buffalo, herd after herd, and camped on a little creek putting out from the mountains. There for some days they had good success, the hunters killing fat cows faster than the women could handle them.

"One evening Weasel Moccasin stood outside the lodge; the sun was setting, and just before it went down it seemed to split into a thousand parts, sending bright-colored rays flashing in every direction. 'It is a sign,' he said aloud, 'that tomorrow I shall meet my death. Somewhere on the plain, in some way, I know not how, my body will grow cold before the sun goes down again.'

"His aunt, busy inside preparing the evening meal, heard his words, came out and scolded him: 'Go in at once and sit down,' she said. 'You have no right to think such things; you are not well. This very night I will prepare some of my herb water, and you shall drink it.'

"'I need it not,' he replied. 'I am not sick. Pay no heed to my words. I know not why I said it, and yet, surely that is a sign of approaching death.'

"'True,' said his aunt, 'it is the sign, but why for you any more than for any of the rest of us here, or for some one back in the main camp? Come in now, and eat.'

"Early the next morning the hunters started out again, riding eastward and some distance before they sighted a herd of buffalo. Then they separated to surround it, Weasel Moccasin riding ahead slowly with his uncle, Big Plume, in order to give the others time to make the circle. Suddenly, from a knoll ahead of them, four Assiniboines jumped up and ran for a coulee further on. My cousin had a swift horse, the fastest of all our people's herds, and in no time he was upon them. Twice he fired, and each time one of the enemy fell dead. The other two had separated, and he rode down upon one of them regardless of the bullets which were whizzing by him. Suddenly the Assiniboine ceased firing, his cartridges apparently all expended, and disdaining to shoot, Weasel Moccasin raised his gun as a club, to brain the enemy. Alas! At that very moment the Assiniboine drew an old pistol and shot him through the body. The next instant he was felled by my cousin's blow, and his shadow went to join those of his companions along their dreary trail.

"Big Plume came hurrying up, as did the others. 'I am shot,' said the warrior; 'help me get to camp.'

"Big Plume got up behind and supported him, and the little party started for the camp. Some of the others were anxious to follow and kill the remaining Assiniboine, but the wounded man forbade it. 'Let him return to his people,' he said, 'and tell them that the Piegans killed his companions.'

"Very slowly they rode toward camp, and their hearts were heavy. The wounded one became weaker and weaker; blood oozed from his lips; he reeled to and fro in his uncle's strong arms. They came to a deep coulee and were sheltered from the wind. 'Help me down,' he said, 'I am dying.'

"Gently they laid him down, spreading their robes and blankets for his couch, and saying to his uncle: 'Pity and care for my family,' he breathed his last. His words had come true; the sign had foretold his death.

"Well do I remember the hunting party's return. They came riding slowly and silently over the hill, and we all stood by our lodges instead of running to meet them, for we felt that they brought sad news. We saw that their faces were painted black, their hair unbound and streaming in the wind. Then presently the word spread through camp, 'Weasel Moccasin is dead; but before he fell he killed three Assiniboines.' The women wailed, the warriors shouted his name in praise, and for a long, long time the whole camp mourned. They had brought his body, and that day we buried him, wrapping him in choice robes and lashing him on a platform in his lonely lodge, with all his weapons by his side. And near about three of his favorite horses were shot, that their shadows might accompany him on his lonely road to the Sandhills. As soon as this was done, we struck camp and moved southeast to Middle Creek. But the people sorrowed; they could not forget his untimely end. All that long winter there was no more dancing nor singing in the camp."*

*The following version of Weasel Moccasin's death is recorded in C. C. Uhlenbeck, "Original Blackfeet Texts," *Verhandelingen der Koninklijke Akademie van Welenschappen te Amsterdam, Afleeling Letterkunde* (Amsterdam, 1911), XII, 71: "Towards the spring of 1879 they left the camp for a buffalo-hunt, taking many horses and small lodges with them. They were accompanied by the women. During a night the Sioux made a raid on them, and stole horses. Chief Big-plume (O'maxsapop) led the Piegans to chase the Sioux. They overtook the Sioux on Beaver creek. There were seven Sioux. Weasel-moccasin and his followers ran after these Sioux, he himself being on a swift horse before them all. When Weasel-moccasin was near the Sioux, he dismounted to fight. He soon got shot about the heart, and died on the way to camp. The Piegans killed six of the seven Sioux. One Sioux escaped."

V

THE name of our camping place, Sturgeon Island, reminded us that we had promised a medical friend the head and skin of a sturgeon, a most repulsive-looking and ill-flavored fish. Accordingly, we put out a line of well-baited hooks from the stern of the boat, but found them intact in the morning. Sturgeon, cat and other fish of the Upper Missouri are rarely caught later than September, and it is said they go far downstream to winter.

We got an early start from this camp, leaving the island before we could well see the channel; but I knew that there were no rapids for many a mile to come, and there would be no difficulty in getting off a shoal should we happen to run aground. There was some fog on the water which for a time enabled us to get quite close to numerous flocks of ducks and geese before they raised, but I was too busy rowing to keep warm to try for a shot. Sah-né-to, muffled in various cloaks and shawls, was shivering until the sun finally appeared and cast its welcome rays into the valley. Three miles below Sturgeon Island the valley suddenly widens out and the slopes are more gentle, the south one supporting several pine groves of large extent. Just where the semi-canyon ends a splendid grove capping a hill quite near the river tempted me ashore, for I felt sure that it sheltered some deer. When we landed the bar was all cut up by their sharp hoofs, and, alas! for my plans, there were also the tracks of a good-sized grizzly deeply sunk in the mud. Sah-né-to saw them before she got quite out of the boat and promptly returned to her place in the stern. There was no need for me to ask why. "If you are afraid," I said, "come with me. I believe I can find a buck up there in the timber."

She shook her head and looked away across the river.

"Well, then," I continued, "you stay here and let me go; if a bear should happen along, you can push out into the stream."

"You well know," she replied, "that I cannot handle the oars. Let us go on; we still have a little meat and the goose. There are plenty of deer ahead."

We went on. Sah-né-to is very much afraid of bears. Not that she has ever had any experience with them; her people tell some wonderful tales of their ferocity and cunning, and, of course, she believes them all. Another mile brought us to the mouth of Snake Creek, entering the river through a long, wide, sagebrush flat. Up its barren valley, away to the north, we got a glimpse of the pine-clad buttes and bluffs near its source, where there are great numbers of mule deer. Although this stream is named Snake Creek, I doubt the rattlers being more plentiful in its vicinity than elsewhere in these badlands; they are pretty evenly distributed and very numerous. We saw none, as they had gone into their "dens" for the winter.

Five miles below this point we came to Cow Creek, or Middle Creek, as Sah-né-to calls it, the mention of which the night before had prompted her reminiscences of other days. I also have some reminiscences of the place, for it was here that I got one of the bad scares of my life. We had run out of blankets down at our Carroll trading post, and with an English half-blood named John Hudson, I was sent up to the mouth of the Judith to procure as many as possible from another trader.

The up trip was uneventful. On our way we camped one night in the Cow Island bottom in one of the best fortified cabins I ever saw. It had bastions and loopholes, and was connected with an Indian-proof stable by an underground passageway. Its owners had deserted it and we took possession for the time. We were successful in getting all the blankets our two small, home-made sleds would hold, and started back. About four o'clock we came to Snake Creek and noticed a great many buffalo moving uneasily about the flat and crossing the river to the south side. As we went on they became more plentiful, great herds thundering down the hills from the north, crossing over and rushing madly up the south side of the valley. Occasionally we heard the booming of guns. A couple of weeks before this some Assiniboines had wantonly killed a woodhawk named Koontz, and his friends having caught two of the murderers, promptly strung them up to the nearest tree. Consequently, there was bad blood between that tribe and the whites. This was a favorite hunting ground with the Assiniboines and we concluded that they were the people behind the flying buffalo. "If we can only reach that cabin, John," I said, "we can stand 'em off."

"Yes," he replied, "if we can only get there first. Let's pound 'em on the back."

And we did. We were still two miles from the cabin by the shortest cut, which was to leave the winding river and strike directly across the flat. We found a place to get up the bank, and then lashed our ponies into a dead run, and the way we bounced through and over the sagebrush must have been a sight. But long before we got to the cabin a number of mounted Indians came down out of the hills between it and us, and our haven of refuge was cut off. We slackened our gait at once. There was no possibility of our running them, so outwardly bold, but inwardly very badly scared, we kept on our course. "If it wasn't for these blankets," John said, "they might possibly let us go; but when they see them 'twill be all day with us."

The Indians were quite near us by this time, and I picked up my Winchester, cocked it, and laid it across my knees. I can't say what my thoughts were, except that I was afraid, and at the same time angry. I decided to shoot at the first hostile movement on their part. They were now within a few yards. I was not looking at their faces, but at their rifles slung across the pommels of their saddles, when a brown hand was outstretched toward me, and I heard a familiar voice say: "How! How! Appekunny."

I could hardly believe my eyes. Why, 'twas my old friend Red-Bird's-Tail sitting there on his horse and grinning. I jumped off my sled and shook hands with him. "John," I said to my wondering companion, "we are safe; these are my old friends, the Piegans." He gave a long sigh of relief. "I thought," he said, "that I would never see my old woman any more."

So instead of being shot and furnishing material for a scalp dance, we camped with friends that night, for the whole tribe was just behind the chief and the few that rode with him, and the flat was soon dotted with their lodges and horse herds. From one place we were called to another to feast on pemmican, stewed berries, broiled tongues and other Indian delicacies, and we ate so much that we could not sleep when bedtime came. During the evening Red-Bird's-Tail asked why we were going so fast when they first saw us, and I coolly lied and said that we were cold and hurrying to the cabin to get warm. It will never do to let an Indian think you know such a thing as fear. I tried to get the tribe to accompany us down the river, expatiating upon the large herds of buffalo and other game in the vicinity of our post. "The Crees are with you," they replied, "also there is much liquor. We would drink and quarrel with them, and, while we can whip them, many good lives here would be uselessly wasted. Tomorrow we cross here for the headwaters of the Yellow River."

In the days of river transportation few steamboats went above this point after the June raise had passed, as the river was too swift and shallow for them. Cargo was unloaded here and taken overland by large "bull" and mule freighting outfits to Fort Benton and the mining camps beyond. A book might be written about the adventures of the freighters along the trail. War parties always infested it, and sometimes got the scalps and plunder they were seeking.

It was near the mouth of this creek that the Nez Perces crossed the Missouri on their memorable march across a part of Washington and Idaho, under the leadership of Chief Joseph in 1877. At the time a few soldiers and citizens, a dozen men in all, were guarding some Government freight. They saw the Indians crossing and lost no time in preparing for the worst, digging breastworks and making barricades of sacks of flour. At sundown the Indians opened fire from the hills, only a couple of hundred yards distant, and twice during the night charged the camp, but were driven back with serious loss each time, the whites losing only one man. In the morning the whole tribe pulled out disgusted, only to fall into the hands of General [Nelson A.] Miles a few days later. Some distance up Cow Creek they plundered a large freight outfit, taking such goods as they wanted and burning the rest with the wagons and harness. The freighters managed to escape by good luck and hard riding.

We beached the Good Shield at the mouth of Cow Creek, and going up on the flat sought in vain for the fortified cabin; not a stick of it remained. Then we climbed the rocky buttes, where the Nez Perces had opened fire on the freight guards. Here and there we found many small piles of rocks behind which they had cached, and numerous cartridge shells of .50, .45, and .44 caliber. We took a few of the shells as a memento of the place, and then returned to the boat.

A mile farther on, and half a mile below the mouth of Calf Creek, another small stream coming in from the north, I pointed out to Sah-né-to the place where I had fired my last shot at buffalo. On our way down the river the morning after camping with the Piegans, I noticed a yearling standing alone in the sagebrush and shot it. I distinctly heard the bullet thud into it, but the animal never flinched nor moved, and I was about to shoot again when it suddenly collapsed and fell in its tracks. Whether or not I had a premonition that it was my last buffalo, with John's aid I skinned it intact, leaving the horns and hoofs on the hide. Later I had it tanned and gaudily painted, Indian fashion, and sent it to an Eastern friend for safe keeping. He has it yet, and after all these years it is his by rights.

At the head of Cow Island, a few hundred yards down, we had no little difficulty in finding enough water to carry us over the shoal, which extends from it clear across to the north shore. What channel there is runs parallel with it, and about fifty feet from the shore. We saw many deer tracks on its sandy bars, whitetail, of course, as the mule deer do not live in the timbered bottoms and islands, coming down to the river only when in need of water.

The general course of the river along here is south of east. A mile or so below Cow Island, however, it turns sharply west of south, rounds a high, narrow ridge and then turns back east of north, making a bend of five miles, which is only a mile across. The south side of the valley around the bend is densely timbered, and at the heads of the coulees are cut walls of sandstone, of a much darker color than that above the mouth of the Judith. There should be some mountain sheep up among the rocks and breaks, and the timber certainly shelters many deer, for we saw their trails leading down to the shore.

Passing the bend, we came to Dry Island, so named because the passage between it and the south shore has filled up, water now standing only in pools, where once was a deep channel. It was time for lunch, and we went ashore, looking around a little before we sat down to eat. We had both seen some deer sign during our wanderings, but nothing to equal that we found here. Around the pools of dead water, and the whole length of the alternately muddy and sandy old channel, there wasn't a place as large as one's hand that did not bear the impression of a deer's foot. Most of them were made by mule deer, but there were also numbers of whitetail tracks. Back from the channel is a high cut bank at the edge of the flat, and at each place it could be climbed the deer had made a wide dusty trail.

While sitting on the bow of the boat eating our lunch, a whitetail doe and her fawns came out of the timber and several hundred yards below us, and after drinking fed around on the shore for some time. The fawns were in high spirits, and did some bucking and kicking which would have made a broncho ashamed of himself. We did not molest them, and they finally went quietly back into the brush. It was here, after lunch, that we found the first signs of a disease which had killed many whitetail deer during the summer.

In a small open park in the timber lay a magnificent buck, in the willows a fawn, and on the outer shore a two-year-old doe. The two latter had been dead a long time, the buck not more than three weeks. What this disease was no one has been able to tell with certainty. It was local, extending, so far as I could learn, only from Cow Island to the mouth of the Fourchette, one hundred miles by river, and did not affect the mule deer at all. Mr. Jas. Gibson, who has lived on the river for thirty years, claims that it was not a disease, but that the mortality was caused by eating the bulb of a weed which is poisonous. The leaves of the plant are not poisonous, and in ordinary years, he says, the bulb is so firmly imbedded in the soil that in eating the leaves the deer do not pull it up and eat it too. This season, however, was exceptionally wet and rainy, and as a consequence many deer died from eating it, as they easily pulled up the whole plant. For proof, Mr. Gibson cited the wet summer of 1886, when many whitetail died the same way.

The only post-mortem I heard of was made by Mr. Mark Frost, a rancher who lives near the mouth of the Musselshell River. Out hunting one day, he shot two fawns, which slowly rose up out of the sagebrush and stood stupidly staring at him. When he came to cut them open, he found that their milt was congested and that their stomachs contained a viscid, ill-smelling, yellowish fluid. He did not take the meat. The mortality began in June, and ended in October with the drying of the plants and other growths from the effect of frost, another point which seems to sustain Mr. Gibson's theory. Whatever the cause, the deer died very suddenly after being taken sick, as evidenced by the good condition of those found. Anthrax is the only disease known which kills so suddenly, and had it been that, the mule deer, bighorn, antelope and cattle along the river would get it, too.

Leaving our lunching place, we pushed off, and a stretch of swift water took us quickly down around a bend and in sight of Crescent and Grand Islands. We arrived at the head of the latter about one o'clock, and having made twenty-five miles since daylight, decided to camp. This is one of the largest islands on the river, a mile and a half long and half a mile wide. At its upper end there is a magnificent grove of tall old cottonwoods, and a growth of smaller timber completely belts it. The rest of the island is a level plain, covered with buck brush and tall grasses. We soon had the tent up under a large cottonwood, and then proposed a hunt up in the breaks of the south side of the valley, for mule deer. There were numerous tracks and trails of whitetail where we were, also more wolf signs than in any place we had yet seen, but after finding the dead deer on Dry Island, we did not care especially for that kind of meat.

Directly opposite the island a long high-cut bank shuts off
sight of anything beyond it. After crossing the river we were
obliged to walk up the shore some distance to find a place
where we could climb it, but when we did finally arrive on the
summit, a typical view of the badlands country was spread
out before us; long ridges and deep coulees sloping up for
miles; hills of blue clay absolutely devoid of vegetation; here
and there patches of juniper brush and groves of pine, especially in the heads of the coulees, and back of them cut walls
of sandstone. We started up the nearest ridge, following a
well-beaten game trail. After traveling a mile or more we
stopped to rest a bit, and I caught sight of a deer as it was
entering a pine grove at the head of a short lateral coulee not
far away. We were not long in getting to the lower edge of it,
but there was so much underbrush that I did not like to go in,
fearing that I would scare the animal out without getting sight
of it; so I decided to circle around to the upper edge of the
timber and have Sah-né-to try to drive it to me. Another
climb of half a mile and I stood on the top of a high cliff; at
its foot there was a boulder-strewn slope of some fifty yards,
and then the pines. I waved my hat to Sah-né-to, saw her
start into the timber, and then sat down to await the result
of my plan.

In order to have this story read right, I suppose I ought to
make my pencil say that the deer suddenly bounded out of
the timber several hundred yards away and ran as fast as it
could, and that at the crack of my trusty rifle it gave a con-
vulsive spring and fell dead. What really did happen was this:
I had been looking over the ridges and groves to my left, trying to spot some game, and again turning my attention to the
business in hand, was surprised to see five deer, one of them a
good-sized buck, standing on the slope right under me and
looking curiously into the timber from which they had likely
just emerged. Back and forth they swung their great ears, and

occasionally stamped the ground with their forefeet. I allow that it was unfair, but we needed meat, and I took a careful sight on the buck's back just back of its withers and dropped him. The others made a few jumps, but did not know which way to run, until I threw a rock at them and shouted, when they hurried away along the edge of the timber and turned up the nearest coulee.

I was obliged to go back several hundred yards to get around the end of the cliff, and by the time I got to the fallen deer Sah-né-to appeared a little further on. She said she had heard the deer run when she scared them up, and remarked that she had found an old "war house."

The buck was larger than I thought when I saw him from the cliff, and still very fat, for the rutting season had barely commenced. He was too heavy to be packed whole, so I skinned out the forequarters and hung them on the nearest tree. But before starting back the "war house" had to be inspected. It stood in the thickest part of the timber, and was a large one, some sixteen feet in diameter inside. Like all others of its kind, 'twas built of a number of long poles set up cone shape. The many layers of pine and balsam boughs which had covered it had long since slipped down and decayed, and the flooring of brush was in a like condition. We poked around inside where the warriors had sat and slept, hoping to find some little trinket they had lost or forgotten, but all we found were mice-gnawed ribs of deer or mountain sheep. There are hundreds of these "war houses" hidden in the breaks of the Missouri, or rather, there were. Most of them have fallen down and rotted away. They were built by parties of Indians on the warpath in order to screen the flame of their fire from observant eyes, and also as a protection from the cold and storms. We wondered what tribe had built this one, where they were bound, and what had been their success. More than likely they had their eyes on some woodhawk's little band of horses, and perchance secured them and his scalp also.

Although I packed but half the deer, my back and shoulders ached before I finally dropped it in the boat. There was ample time to get in the remainder before dark, but Sah-né-to rightly said that there were other days. So we rowed across to camp.

After dinner I set out to explore the island, walking down through the center to its lowest point. Trails of the whitetail were everywhere, and at every step I expected to see some of the animals jump up, for their many beds in the grass and low buck brush showed that they passed a part of their time in the open. Then I remembered the wolf trails on the shore. Wolves know the runways of game as well as human lovers of the chase, and better. Here, for instance, unless they were to swim the river, deer cross to and from the island only at its head, where a shallow, gravelly ford separates it from the north shore. All along behind it the sluggish water has a bottom of fathomless soft mud, which they do not attempt to cross. Knowing this, the wolves secure their prey by watching the runway, while several of their companions drive the island. All the way down, and back by the north shore, I never saw a deer. Where the runway crossed the sandy bar and entered the water were the imprints of flying feet, both deer and wolves. Could I have crossed over I doubt not that I would have found some freshly gnawed bones and bits of hide.

At the lower point of the island I found some recent beaver cuttings, and also some moccasin tracks in the mud. From the shape of the latter I knew that they were of Cree make, and concluded that there was a camp of Crees somewhere in the vicinity. Alas, for the beaver. They have been protected by law for a long time, but every year their number grows less and less.

VI

SOON after daylight the next morning we discovered eleven mule deer walking along under the cut bank on the opposite side of the river. One of them was a very large buck, and had an immense set of antlers. They picked their way down the shore, waving their great ears, occasionally stopping to look about, and at last disappeared up a deep coulee.

After breakfast I brought the remainder of the deer I had killed down to camp, and then we loaded up and set sail, a good wind having started from the west. Here at Grand Island the really well-timbered bottoms of the Missouri begin; the stream flows from one side of the valley to the other like the course of a snake, and in every bend a growth of cottonwoods and willows extends a part or all of the way back to the foot of the valley slope. Here also one first begins to see the "sawyers," for which the river is famous, and which have sunk many a good boat. The current ever encroaching upon the soft soil of the bottoms, especially the upper, or western sides, is continually eating them away; a great piece of undermined ground falls into the stream, and with it one or more trees, roots and all. Down goes the tree to the bottom, its top rising several feet above the surface of the water and slanting with the current. Then the spring rush of ice cuts away its limbs, shaves and sharpens the trunk, and the sand and sediment deeply embedding its roots hold it immovably in place like a great lance. If the tip is just beneath the surface, a swirl and rippling of the water reveals its presence. But the most observant of pilots cannot always detect one, and with a crash the boat is impaled, and a few moments later sinks beneath the muddy tide.

Wonderful, almost unbelievable, is the amount of soil and sand annually carried away and shifted by this river. The finest of it is held in suspension and is finally deposited in the Gulf of Mexico. The coarsest is cut away here, deposited there, picked up and shifted again, each time a little further downstream. In one day the ever-shifting channel will remove all traces of a long, wide bar or island several feet in height. Often, as we rowed or sailed along, we could see them melting away, yards and yards at a time, and great chunks of the bottom, ten, twenty, even thirty feet in height, were continually falling in with a resounding splash. The careful navigator will do well to keep out from the cut banks. Where a bottom wears away, the bottom on the opposite side fills out, and at a rate which can be accurately measured by the growth of the trees. Always at the outer edge are cottonwood and willow sprouts; back of them belt after belt of timber, each one larger than the other by a year's growth, until finally one comes to the full-grown trees, tall, rough-barked and wide of girth. The river once shifting and leaving an ever-widening bar, the wash from the hills raises it layer by layer. A moderate rainstorm will deposit several inches of the badland soil upon it, a big storm as much as a foot. In the rainy season, and when the winter snows are melting under the influence of the warm spring sun, the steep coulees are miniature torrents, carrying the soil and sticky clays down not only in solution, but in balls from several inches up to three feet in diameter. Here and there at the mouths of these coulees one can often see several hundred of them stranded by the receding waters.

The scenery this morning was not especially impressive, merely a succession of bars, broken ridges and deep coulees on the north side of the valley, and only a few pine groves on the southern slope. A run of five miles brought us to the Two Calf Islands, at the mouth of Two Calf Creek, which flows into the river from the south. These are old names, bestowed by some of the early voyageurs, but why, tradition does not say. The islands, separated only by a narrow strip of deep water, are small and covered with timber. There were several beaver slides on the lower one, but no fresh sign; evidently the moccasined trapper had been here also. On a high bank near the mouth of the creek stands an old-time hunter's cabin in a fair state of preservation, even to the rawhide door. Its dimensions are about twelve by fourteen feet, and the great, rude, rough, stone fireplace and chimney at its rear take up a large share of the space.

The breeze freshened and we ran the six miles from this point to the mouth of Armell's Creek in an hour. This is a fair-sized stream, heading near the Black Butte, thirty miles south. The latter part of its course is between high, rough, pine-clad hills. It was named after Charles Armell, a trader for the American Fur Company, who once managed a branch post here for some time. Sah-né-to said that her people called this creek It-tsis-ki-ot-sop—Crushed, or, more liberally, Trapped. Somewhere along its course, in the long ago, she said, the Piegans were camping and hunting, and some one discovered a seam of soft, red ochre, or burnt clay, in a high cut bank. The news quickly spread through camp and created great excitement, for the substance was not common, and in great demand for making a sacred paint for the face. In other words, 'twas great medicine. Early the next morning more women flocked to the place than could work at it at one time, for the seam was not long. They dug and gouged and scraped with such implements as they had, sharp-pointed sticks and shoulder blades of buffalo, and had mined in for a considerable distance when a large portion of the high bank fell, completely burying twenty-seven of them and seriously injuring several more. All of the twenty-seven were dead when the people finally uncovered them.

We expected to find an old friend named King located at

the mouth of this stream, but found his ranch on the next bottom below. We landed quietly and slipped along through a grove of trees to the house unobserved. Then Sah-né-to sprang out and addressed Mrs. King in her own language, greatly to the latter's surprise and delight. They had not seen each other for more than a year, when King and his family had left the foot of the Rockies to locate here. I asked him what he thought of the country.

"Say," he replied, "I find that I've just thrown away the twenty years and more I put in buffeting the cold winds up where you are. Here the wind doesn't blow; see how straight and tall these cottonwoods are? Those on your place are bent and dwarfed. Up there you have to rustle hard all summer to get enough hay to winter your stock. Here we don't need any. Cattle find ample feed and shelter here in these bottoms and keep fat during the worst of winters."

He was right.

Game, Dick said, was abundant. There were a few elk and grizzly bears up on Armell's Creek, plenty of mule deer in the breaks, several bands of antelope on the nearby plains. There were some whitetail in the bottoms, but many had died during the summer. He had found eight in the timber nearby. "But," he continued, "this isn't going to last; there is a Cree half-blood outfit living on the next bottom below here, and last winter they killed over two hundred deer, to say nothing of other game. In the fall all they bought to winter on was twenty sacks of flour; no bacon, no beans, no sugar, nothing else. So you may know that they came pretty near living on meat straight. Of course, they couldn't have eaten two hundred deer; they kill a large number for their skins and for wolf baits. I saw a great many carcasses they had poisoned. Yes, they've pretty well cleaned up the beaver about here. I saw the old man floating by on a raft yesterday, and he had something covered with his blankets; beaver skins, I suppose."

I remarked that I had found moccasin tracks around some beaver workings not far above.

The Kings insisted that we should remain with them a week at least. But winter was due at any time, and much as we would have liked to accept their hospitality, we pushed on the next morning. Passing the location of the Cree half-bloods, we saw the patriarch of them all squatting upon his heels at the edge of the bank, ragged, unkempt, black of skin, his long hair cut square around like a mop. I felt like trying the effect of a square-nosed bullet upon his anatomy. "Dogface!" said Sah-né-to, "why has the Great Father forbidden my people to make further war upon them? They were ever our warriors' legitimate prey. They have no place, no right in this country."

A strong breeze was blowing again this morning, and we made the eleven miles to the mouth of Little Rocky Creek in less than two hours. This stream heads in the Little Rocky Mountains, twenty-five miles north of the river. Hunting buffalo on its headwaters once with the noted shot, Eli Guardipee, we found in a park in the foothills two large bull elk, their antlers firmly interlocked. They had been dead so short a time that the wolves had not touched them. For many yards around them the turf had been tramped so that scarce a blade of grass was left, and there they must have stood for days, suffering agonies from thirst and want of food, although the grassy plain was all around them and the cool mountain stream but a few yards distant. We cut off their heads, of course, antlers and all, and got them into the post on a hastily constructed sledge. Ultimately they came into the possession of Dr. C. Hart Merriam, who has kindly loaned them to the National Museum in Washington.

From the mouth of Little Rocky Creek a further sail of eight miles brought us to the Carroll bottom, where we had held forth in other days. I could hardly recognize the place.

Where our post had once stood was now the north side of the river, and several hundred yards back in the brush and young cottonwoods, which had grown up in the nineteen years since we had abandoned it. We lowered the sail and went ashore. Midway in the bottom a coulee comes in from the distant breaks, and at its mouth I had once killed some buffalo. "We will go over there," I said to Sah-né-to, "and take a couple of the skulls. I would like to keep them as a memento of old times."

Well I remember that hazy, smoky morning in the rutting season, when, arising soon after daylight, I heard the moaning of the impassioned bulls back in the breaks. No one in the post was astir. The few lodges of Crees and Blackfeet nearby were silent. I picked up my rifle, thrust a handful of extra cartridges into my pocket and slipped over to the coulee, meeting the herd just this side of it. Some of the animals ran back in the direction whence they came; others dashed down into the deep coulee and up the steep trail on the other side, which would admit of but one climbing at a time. There, just as they gained the opposite level, I dropped nine of them, bulls and cows. The last one was a cow, and when it fell its calf stopped and stood by it, and butted it in the side in a vain attempt to reach the teats. Then I hated myself. At least, I thought, the meat shall not be wasted, and returning to the lodges I routed the occupants out and told them to butcher the animals and divide the meat and hides as they saw fit.

Arriving at the coulee, we crossed it and a glance over the ground convinced us that we would not find what we sought. To say nothing of skulls, not even a bone was left to show that a buffalo had ever fallen there. The wash from the hills had buried them, or, perchance, they had been shipped by some gatherer of bones ere the steamers ceased running on the upper river. We retraced our steps and sat down near the boat to eat our lunch.

The pleasantest years of my life were passed at this place. From September until spring thousands of Indians, Bloods, Blackfeet and Crees, were continually coming and going, coming in to trade their robes and furs, going out to hunt for more. One winter we traded for a few more than four thousand robes, seven hundred raw hides, twenty-three hundred small skins—elk, deer and antelope—six hundred wolf and coyote pelts and some three hundred beaver skins. Also for great quantities of pemmican and dried meat. I forget the weight, but remember that it was stacked up in long piles like cordwood. That was the winter we got the spotted robe.

The animal, an unusually large cow buffalo, was killed by a young Blackfoot one day when Mr. Jos. Kipp, the owner of our trading outfit, happened to be in the camp. When skinned and spread out on the ground, the hide was found to have a border of pure white a foot deep all around. The head and tail were also white, and there was a large, round, white spot on each flank. The young hunter gave it to his father and mother, and they promised Mr. Kipp that he should have it in due time. The old woman tanned it as soft as ever a robe was tanned, and the old man painted upon the flesh side in brilliant colors the record of his battles, his "coups," and wonderful medicines. Then the proud couple brought it in and showed it to us, and also to two rival traders. "Be not afraid," they said to us, "we promised you the robe, and will do as we say; but we will keep it a little while."

Both of the other traders wanted it, of course, and for weeks and weeks kept the old people supplied with whisky and tobacco and other things prized by the Indians. And each one of them was sure that he was going to get it, and bragged about it; but both were pilgrims, and did not know the red man's ways. One day in the spring, true to their word, the old couple came in and threw the robe over our counter. "There 'tis," the old man said, "tomorrow we start for the

North. We've had a real good time with it."

We gave them about fifty dollars worth of goods. A month later a Montreal man traveling through the country heard of the robe, had the steamer he was on stop at our place and bought it. I wonder if he still has it? Does any Montreal reader know some one who has a spotted robe?

The Indians seldom traded after nightfall, but on winter evenings our trade room was a general lounging place for the chiefs and old men, and many an interesting tale they told as they sat around the stove and smoked and supped the spirits we occasionally set out. Tales of war, of the chase, and of their life on the plains. Tales of the doings of their gods, of the creation, of the life hereafter, all of which was interesting to one person at least, who wished to know just what an Indian really thought and believed.

During the long summers, when all furs and robes were valueless, we had nothing to do. The arrival of a steamboat now and then with our mail was the only thing to break the monotony of the days. How often we used to climb to the top of the long hill to look for the smoke rising above the trees away down the valley, which heralded one's approach.

One familiar landmark on the bottom is a gnarled old cottonwood far back of where our trading post once stood; the river has eaten in nearly to its base, and another season it too will topple into the flood. I have good reason to remember it. The "Big-eared White Man," Upham, the old-time trader, was with us. During his long life on the plains he had never killed a buffalo, nor any other game for that matter; he cared nothing for the chase. But one day, seeing an old buffalo bull coming through the bottom, he picked up a .44 carbine and said he guessed he would kill it. Forth he went, and we sat on the shady side of the building and watched him.

The bull was feeding along, and every time it stopped to crop a mouthful of grass he slipped up nearer to it, until he got within fifty or seventy yards of the beast, all unconscious of his approach. Then he raised his carbine and shot it, not through the heart, as he intended, but through the paunch. The next instant, snorting with rage and pain, the bull was after him, and dropping his gun, he ran to the old cotton-wood, grasped its mighty trunk, some four feet in diameter, and frantically tried to climb it, an utter impossibility, of course. On came the bull, and he dodged behind the tree, and for some moments the two played tag around its base, the trader shouting for help, for some one to kill the blankety-blank beast. But the spectators were having too much fun to heed his entreaties until they saw that he was nearly exhausted, and then one of them dropped the bull with a well-directed shot.

Beside the Indians, we did a large trade with the French-Cree half-bloods, who had come from the Saskatchewan, Red River, and other parts of Canada, to follow the buffalo. It was here that their leader, Louis Riel, began preparations for the rebellion of 1885. He was a cold, calculating, suave and educated half-blood, but withal fanatical and lacking in good, plain sense. There was a Jesuit priest with us, and both he and others told Riel that his handful of men could not possibly whip the Canadian troops, to say nothing of the thousands Great Britain would put into the field if necessary. "You do not understand," he would reply. "We are like the children of Israel of old, a persecuted race. God is with us, and will lead us to a great and glorious victory."

A few years later the Red Coats hung him.*

There were then some wild and desperate men here in these badlands, especially Big-Nose George and Dutch John's

---

*See Joseph Kinsey Howard, *Strange Empire* (New York, 1952) for an excellent treatment of Louis Riel and the French half-blood, or Metís, rebellions against Canada.

gangs of horse thieves and murderers. Just where their strong-
holds were we never asked nor learned. They occasionally
came to our post and purchased provisions, and we always
felt relieved when they departed. Most likely the reason they
never held us up was that they knew we seldom kept any cash
on hand, our trade being almost entirely in robes and furs.
And again, they had to obtain provisions somewhere, and we
sold to them and asked no questions. We didn't dare to.

One day a member of one of these gangs was standing in
the doorway of our post as a young Cree and his wife were
sauntering by. "See me plunk the Indian," he said, and level-
ing his "gun," he shot the poor fellow through the kidneys.
It was well for him that the Crees were all out after buffalo
at that time!

The priest ministered to the poor Indian's spiritual wants,
and I filled him up with whisky to relieve the pain, and we
gave him the best send off we could; but for many a day I
could not forget the cruel act. That was the only Indian I ever
saw killed in cold blood.

About two o'clock, having finished our lunch, we again set
sail and ran around the point of the bottom, past the heavy
growth of timber and willows, where I once had another
experience with buffalo one day. We were out of meat, there
were no Indians around, so I was appointed to furnish some.
I sallied forth down the bottom to look for deer, and was
walking along the edge of the timber, when I saw a buffalo
cow pass into a growth of thick willows, and out of sight before I could shoot. I followed, and presently saw her rubbing
against a tree, and promptly dropped her where she stood.
But I wasn't prepared for the effect of the shot. Unknown to
me, there were several hundred buffalo out on the shore of
the river, and at the crack of the rifle they came rushing back
pell-mell through the willows, regardless of trails. I had barely
had time to get behind a small cottonwood, when they began

to rush by, many so close that I could have reached out and touched them, but I hugged the tree and kept mum and in a minute they all passed. The way they tore down brush and crashed through the thick willows was something remarkable. Had I not, fortunately, been close to a tree, it is likely they would have trampled me into the earth.

It was here, too, that my friend Guardipee had a close call from a grizzly. He had been down the valley hunting, and was returning with a big mule deer fastened on behind his saddle, when he ran across a big bear at the edge of the timber and shot it. Although the bullet pierced its lungs, the bear took after him, and the pony, handicapped by its heavy load, could not get over the ground nearly as fast as the enraged animal. Eli had time to fire but once, missing, when the bear was right at the pony's heels, and with a swipe of its claws badly lacerated one of its haunches and legs; but luckily Eli's next shot struck the animal fairly in the brain, and the short, but exciting, run was over. It was the largest female grizzly I ever saw, and very fat. We got twelve gallons of oil from it.

We soon passed the familiar place which had revived so many memories of other days, and turning a bend bid it good-bye. For the rest of the afternoon the wind was changeable, and we finally tied up at Ryan's Island, named after an old woodhawk, and camped, having made twenty-seven miles since leaving King's ranch.*

*From this point onward the Missouri River presently flows into Fort Peck Reservoir. The river, the bottomlands, and the breaks and coulees that Schultz subsequently describes no longer exist. Proposals have been made to inundate the river from Cow Creek to Fort Benton, forever destroying the last wild stretch of the scenic and historic Missouri River.

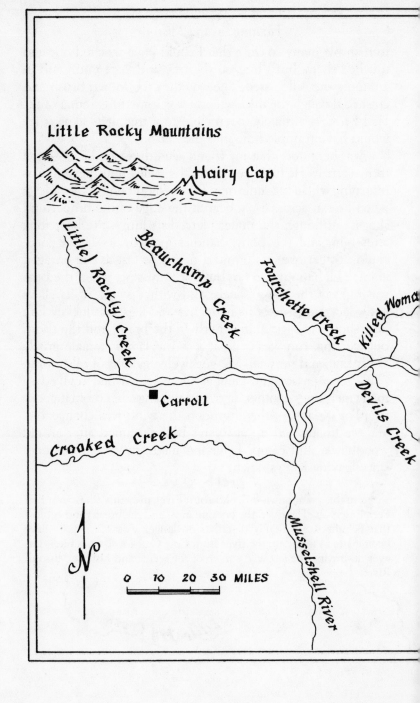

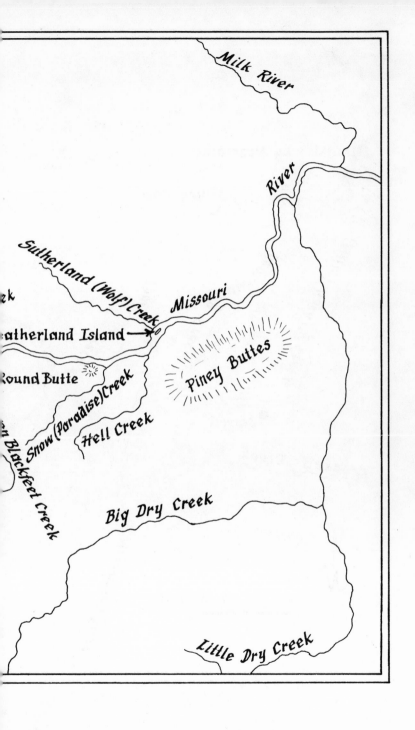

VII

WE left Ryan's Island at sunup. There was a heavy fog hanging over the water and filling the valley, and for an hour or more we simply drifted with the current, not caring to risk striking a sawyer or sunken rock while running at full speed. As it was, we hit a sunken log and lost the hindquarters of our buck, which, to better balance the boat, I had placed on the little deck on the bow in front of the mast. It went overboard with a splash, and that was the last we saw of it, for the water was deep. Sah-né-to felt worse about it than I did, and gave me a scolding for not tying the saddle to the mast. "Well," I said, "it is gone, but not uselessly; it will furnish a feast for your water spirits, and they will be kind to us." She said no more.

There were a great many geese on the bars this morning, as there had been every other morning when there was a heavy fog. I believe they only stop on the river to rest on their way south, and leave very early in the morning, unless there is an unfavorable wind or fog. Of the many thousands we saw on the trip, but one lone goose was feeding, and that was a cripple. I shot it, and was sorry, for there was an old shot wound at the base of the upper mandible, partly healed. Evidently it had half-starved for some time, as it was mere skin and bones, entirely unfit for the table.

When the fog lifted we found ourselves in sight of Hawley Point, a long, narrow bottom on the south side of the river, half a mile across and four miles around by the channel. But to our surprise we found that we were to be saved the four miles, for the river had cut straight across the base of the point in two places, leaving a small island, which was also fast wearing away. All we could see of the old channel was a vast bed of sand, fast growing up with willows and cotton-woods. At the lower end of the island we caught a glimpse of a whitetail deer as it bounded back into the willows. Beau-champ Creek comes into the river at the apex of Hawley Point —that is, when it runs; for the greater part of the year its chan-nel contains water only in places. It heads near the eastern-most butte of the Little Rockies, a very steep, high hill the Blackfeet long ago named Hairy Cap, on account of the dense growth of pines which covers its summit. It used to be an objective point for all the war parties traveling through that part of the country, for they could obtain a view of an im-mense scope of country from its top. Many battles have been fought on and around it between war parties of different tribes.

Except for the heavily timbered bottoms, the scenery along here is uninteresting. The north slope of the valley is barren, and there are few pines on the south slope. Ten miles from Hawley Point the river turns from its generally easterly course sharply to the south, at the base of the long point which ter-minates at the mouth of the Musselshell River, ten miles farther down. From there it runs due north for ten miles, forming a bend only four miles across at the widest place, but twenty miles around. An hour's run brought us to the ranch of our friend, Mark Frost, who has been located on the river for a number of years. We tied up and paid him a short visit. Frost leads an ideal life. He has a fine ranch, a nice band of cattle, which support themselves the year around, and so has absolutely nothing to do but enjoy himself. Once a year he gathers his beef stock and drives them to the railroad, ninety miles distant, ships them to Chicago and purchases a year's supplies, and then back he goes to his ranch. Many persons undoubtedly would call that a lonesome life. He doesn't think so, nor do his good wife and children. Panics may come, banks may break, droughts may ruin the crops of the country, but it makes no difference to him. People will eat beef and he always has it to sell.

Frost is a great hunter, and has a fad for saving the antlers of the game he kills. Strung on the fence near his meat house, and piled on the ground, are antlers of elk, whitetail and mule deer, horns of mountain sheep and antelope. In the house are rugs of the grizzly, mountain lion and wolf, all of his own killing. The lower part of the ranch is heavily timbered and shelters numbers of whitetail deer. Frost said that he only disturbed them once in a great while, when meat was wanted on short notice, and that consequently they were very tame, feeding in sight of the house almost daily. He shoots most of the game he kills up and down the river, or back in the pine breaks, where the mule deer are numerous.

We would have been only too well pleased to accept Frost's invitation to stop and hunt with him a week or two. But our ever-present bugbear of winter and a frozen river prevented. So, after an hour's rest, we went on and arrived at the mouth of the Musselshell in ample time to make camp on the island there. This river heads in the Big Belt and Crazy Mountains, and parallels the Yellowstone for a long way before it turns northward toward the Missouri. A number of tributaries flow into it from the Snowy Mountains. The principal one, Flat Willow Creek, is a beautiful stream; we once had a branch trading post near its mouth.

There have been stirring times here on this Musselshell flat. The shallow ford just below the confluence of the two streams was used by war parties of many tribes on their raids, and even when the river was high they came here to cross, for a war trail between the Missouri and the Yellowstone followed the Musselshell for many miles. Numbers of woodhawks here met their fate in the shape of an Indian arrow or bullet. But there came a day when the redskins paid dearly for the scalps they had taken. A few Yanktonais Sioux had attacked a woodyard, and instead of wiping out the white men as they expected to do, themselves lost several of their party. Back they went to camp somewhere down the river and got up a large party, one hundred and fifty warriors, to revenge their losses. The woodhawks expected they would do this, and in the interval, before their return, managed to collect twenty men at their place to help them. I cannot say just how they managed, but in some way they ambushed the Sioux, killing thirty of them on the ground and driving the remainder into the Missouri, where many more were shot and drowned.* Seventy-two of the party never returned to their lodges. It was in this fight that Liver-eating Johnson got his name. He didn't really eat an Indian's liver, as most persons believe, but ripping a Sioux open he cut off a piece of his liver, held it near his mouth and pretending to take a bite of it said, "Come and help yourselves, fellows, it's good."

Johnson died in California last winter. Another participant in the fight was Daniel Fitzpatrick, who has lived for many years with Mr. Joseph Kipp. He has a bullet wound in the leg which has never completely healed, as a memento of the day. After that experience, Dan says, the Sioux did not molest the woodhawks for a long time.

In the summer of 1884 a few cattlemen fancied that the Missouri badlands sheltered a number of cattle and horse thieves who were preying on their herds, so they got up a gang of cowboys and others under the leadership of one Flopping Bill, and sent them to the river to clean out the bad men. Flopping Bill himself had been a woodhawk, and hadn't the best of reputations. The two notorious gangs of outlaws, Big-Nose George's and Dutch John's, had left the river a year or

*Particulars of this battle may be found in Peter Koch, "Life at Muscleshell in 1869 and 1870." *Contributions to the Montana Historical Society* (Helena, 1896), II, 293–96.

more before this, but the gang had started out to do some hanging, and hang they did many an innocent man along the river. It is said that Flopping Bill had some ancient grudges against a number of them, and took this means to pay them off without danger to his own precious carcass. It is claimed by many that some men were hung for their money and property. At the time a young man named William Downs was located here at the mouth of the Musselshell with his wife. Toward the close of the buffalo trade he had kept a small trading post and woodyard, and was by no means poor. One day the hanging gang rode up to his place and asked him to show them a trail by which they could get out on the prairie to the south. He willingly and innocently mounted his horse and rode away with them, and that was the last that his wife ever saw of him. Somewhere up in the pine breaks they hung or shot him, and buried his body. At the time he had a large sum of money with him. Downs came of a good family somewhere in eastern Canada, and before he came over to the Missouri served a term of years with the Northwest Mounted Police. He was well liked by all who knew him, and was an honest and industrious young man.*

Just before dark, while walking around the island reading the record of the game about, as printed in the sand and mud by their hoofs and paws, I came across a fossil bone of large size, which I thought had been one of the vertebrae of a mastodon. I lugged it to camp, thinking to tell Sah-né-to something of the great animal which roamed here before the glacial period. "Ah!" she said, as I laid it down. "You have the bone of a water bull. Where did you find it?"

I told her, and at the same time concluded not to say any-

*A different assessment of the vigilante action in the Missouri River breaks is offered in Oscar O. Mueller, "The Central Montana Vigilante Raids of 1884," *Montana, the Magazine of Western History*, I, 1 (1951), 23–35.

thing about a mastodon for a while, as from her remark I believed there might be a bit of folk lore forthcoming. So, after the dinner things had been washed and put away, I remarked: "A water bull's bone, is it? Tell me something about the animal; I never saw one."

"Of course you never saw one," she replied. "They died off long, long ago; perhaps hundreds of years. One of them once befriended a man when he was in great trouble. He was a young man named Red Crow, the only son of a poor widow, and he was very much in love with a girl named Two Stars ———"

"And," I interrupted, "there was another man also in love with her, hence the trouble."

"How did you know," she asked, "since you never heard the story?"

"Oh!" I replied, "I guessed; that is about the only thing that makes trouble in this world."

"Well, you were right this time, at least. Another young man named Bull's Head also loved her. His father was a great chief, very rich, and he was pleased when his son told him that he wanted to marry Two Stars, for she was a good girl, very industrious, quite handsome, and her father was a medicine man and quite wealthy.

"The chief went to the medicine man's lodge and they smoked together, talking of various things. Finally the chief came around to the object of his visit. 'What say you,' he asked, 'to giving my son your daughter? He is a good hunter, brave on the war trail for one of his youth, and as he is my only child, all I have will one day fall to him.'

"'Your words are good; pleasant to hear,' said the medicine man, 'and nothing would please me better than what you propose. Alas! the gods have already spoken to me regarding her; recently in my sleep, my secret helper came and said: "You are not to give Two Stars to anyone for a wife until you

78

receive a certain sign, which will be carried by the one we have chosen for her." Also, he told me what the sign would be, but I may not tell you that. I now await it, expecting to see it daily. How nice it would be were your son the chosen one to carry it.'

"The chief went to his lodge, disappointed, of course, yet not angry, for no one questions the ways of the gods. But when Bull's Head was told what the old man had said, he swore that he would have Two Stars in spite of all the gods of the universe, above, below, on the earth and in the water.

"Red Crow and Two Stars had loved each other a long time in secret, and each knew how the other felt, for their eyes had spoken if not their lips. Red Crow was the old medicine man's hunter, and so poor that both knew it would be useless to ask his consent to their union. One day the young man was out hunting deer in the timber, and after a while, sitting down to rest, he absently picked up the soft earth with his stone knive. Something caught the point, and digging a little deeper he uncovered and cut off a small, brown-skinned root, yellow inside, which had a powerful, but pleasant odor, and was good to the taste. He barely touched it with his tongue for fear it was poison. That evening when he returned to camp, he gave it to the old medicine man, and to his great astonishment the latter sprang to his feet, held the root aloft and gave thanks to the gods for their kindness. 'My son,' he said later to the youth, 'you did better than you thought when you brought me this root. I have been expecting it a long time. You shall show me where it grows and its leaf, and you shall have my daughter, for so have the gods decreed.'

"News travels quickly in camp, and when Bull's Head heard that the young couple were soon to marry, he was very angry; he sat long by the fire, scheming, thinking, trying to find some plan to bring the old medicine man's words to naught.

"Two days passed. On the morning of the third day Red

Crow went hunting as usual, although he was to be married that night, for there was to be great feasting and much meat was required. Bull's Head followed and overtook him in the forest. 'Come with me,' he said, 'for I have found a place where game was never hunted and deer are as plentiful as the rabbits here in the brush. Yesterday I made a raft and went to that island you have likely seen away out in the great lake whose shores are not far from here. There I found more game than I ever saw in my life before. Come, let us go; two of us can make the raft go quickly, and we can bring home a big load of meat upon it.'

"Suspecting nothing, thinking his friend's words were true, Red Crow accompanied him. They went through the forest, and after a time came to the lake. There was the raft, two long drift logs lashed together, and they pushed out upon it, paddling hard. They came to the island; its shores were rocky walls standing high above the water's edge, and difficult to climb. 'Go you this way,' said Bull's Head, 'and I will go around the other way, thus will we drive the game to each other.'

"Red Crow started as he was told through the deep woods, and keeping close to the cliffs. He saw no trails, no tracks of deer, no life of any kind except a few small birds in the branches of the trees. 'This is strange,' he said to himself. 'Surely, if there were deer on this island their tracks would be here as well as elsewhere.'

"He kept going, however, on and on, and at last having walked clear around the island, came to the place where they had landed. He shouted for his companion, but there was no answer; he looked for the raft and found it was gone; far, far out on the lake, so far, that he was a mere speck, his companion was paddling it toward the shore and home. Then Red Crow saw light; he remembered that Bull's Head had wished to marry Two Stars and felt sure that he had taken this method to be revenged and marry her after all. His first thought was to make a raft and hurry back, but not a dry stick could he find on the island, not even a piece large enough to support his weight. Dead trees there were, dead and fallen, moss grown and rotten. He sat down on the shore and wept; the distance was far too great to swim, and he despaired of ever seeing home and Two Stars again.

"As he sat there on the rocks grieving, a small duck suddenly swam up close to him and said: 'Why do you grieve? Why are you crying on such a warm, pleasant summer's day?'

"'Oh,' it continued, when the young man had told his troubles, 'and is that all? Cheer up. I will go find one who will aid you,' and it dived beneath the waves.

"Then presently two swans came sailing by on the water and stopped to ask him why he mourned, and they also told him to have courage, that they would find one to aid him. Next came an otter, then a muskrat, proffering aid and hurrying away in search of the promised one. Lastly a beaver came, a very large old beaver, carrying a carefully wrapped bundle which he placed on a rock at the young man's feet. After Red Crow had told him also of his plight, he said:

"'Yes, I heard of this a little while ago from the swans who were talking with you. They were looking for the chief of this lake to get him to carry you home, and he will soon be here. When I heard the way you had been used I took pity, and have brought you a present. In this bundle is a sacred pipe, which we beavers have had for a very long time; take it and keep it, and use it with the sacred prayers and songs I will teach you. Its power is to heal the sick, to give long life, to preserve one from the enemy and make him successful in war.'

"The beaver had just finished teaching Red Crow the songs and prayers, when the duck, the swans, the otter and muskrat were seen approaching them. 'I guess they have found him,' he remarked. The words were no sooner said than a huge animal rose out of the water in front of them with a surge that sent great waves rolling and dashing upon the rocks. The young man started back in fear. 'Don't be afraid,' his friends cried, 'this is the water bull, our chief. Get on his back and he will carry you whence you came.'

"It was a frightful-looking animal, very much larger than a buffalo bull, wearing great horns, wide backed, long, round and fat. But Red Crow took courage, and with his pipe in one hand got astride of it and it started swiftly toward the main shore, swimming the deeper places, wading shallower ones when 'twas still so deep its rider could not see bottom. And so, in a little while, they came to the land, and as soon as Red Crow slid down, the bull turned and went out in the lake without ever having said a word. It was dark when the young man reached camp, and when he entered the old medicine man's lodge he found the people mourning for him, his old mother having already cut off her hair. They thought at first he was a ghost, but after a little, when they had got over their joy and excitement of seeing him alive and well again, they told him that Bull's Head had come into camp and said that while crossing the river in pursuit of a wounded deer his friend Red Crow had been seized by the water people and was likely dead. Then Red Crow told his story to the crowd which had gathered, and when he had finished they ran and seized Bull's Head and killed him. So Two Stars was married to the man she loved after all, and they lived in peace and happiness many years, protected by the sacred pipe. When they died it fell to their son, and ever since it has been kept in the tribe."

"How big do you suppose this water bull was?" I asked.

"'Tis said that when one crossed a river as large as this, its forefeet touched the further shore before its hind ones had come to the water."

Floating on the Missouri

Whether it was the story, or too much dinner, or more than the usual number of smokes, I cannot say; but I do know that just as a monster of the deep had smashed our boat and knocked us into the icy water, I awoke, only too happy to find that I was still on land, and that it was a quarter to one in the morning.

VIII

CROOKED Creek flows into the Musselshell about two miles above the latter's confluence with the Missouri. It is a "dry" stream, water standing in it only in holes, and heads in some ridges bordering Armell's Creek, fifty miles to the west. Its upper course is through a broad plain and then it runs between high pine-clad buttes and ridges where mountain sheep, mule deer and antelope are numerous. I understand that a party of Lewistown, Montana, men who were hunting on the creek a year ago corralled forty deer in a cut wall coulee and killed every one of them, leaving the animals to rot where they fell. Of course they were pilgrims; no old-timer would think of doing such a thing. And they even went home and bragged of the deed and their sportsmanship. Sportsmanship, forsooth.

Years ago, while hunting buffalo on Crooked Creek, I ran across an eccentric character named Thomas Faval, better known as Skunk Cap. He was a north half-blood and spoke English with a broad Scotch accent. But that was not his only language; he spoke Blackfoot, Cree, Crow, Sioux, with equal facility. Wherever he went he carried a staff some seven feet long, to which were fastened various bits of fur and feathers and painted buckskin pouches, all of which he claimed was great medicine, and enabled him to cure all manner of disease. The various Indian tribes all believed in his mysteries, and his services and ceremonies were always in great demand. Consequently he was never short of robes and furs with which to support his three wives, and purchase the rum he so dearly loved. Tom was about seventy-five when I first met him, but still sound and hearty. He was a member of the Sir John Franklin Relief Expedition, and told many interesting stories of his adventures in the far North. He was death on beavers, getting great numbers of them by the aid of his dogs. These were two low, short-legged nondescript fices which he had trained to the business. They would go under water into a bank beaver's hole, follow it up to the den, or living room, and either kill and drag out, or drive out, the occupants. If they were driven out, Tom and his women speared them.

One time at our branch post on Flat Willow Creek we had been out of whisky for some weeks, and Faval, who was camping and trapping nearby, was in despair because his large and ever-increasing pile of beaver skins could not purchase even a dram. But one day our bull train rolled in with supplies, and we were unloading it when Tom happened along. The first thing he noticed was a barrel of whisky standing on the ground, and with triumphant yells he ran up and embraced it, saying, "God bless the puncheon, me b'ys; God bless its generous gairth."*

The Musselshell country is a noted place for fossils of various kinds. I have often heard of a place some twenty miles above its mouth where "one can find almost any kind of an old bone," as our informant said. I once saw a fossilized turtle, found near its mouth by a woodhawk, which measured five feet in length.

The island on which we camped is fast wearing away, the swift current cutting it on both sides. There are some deer on it, and several families of beavers have large caches of winter food at its lower end. May they escape the wiles of the trapper and increase. I would that it were life imprisonment to kill one of them, for it's but little short of taking human life. Long as I have lived in this country, many as have been

*John McDougall, a Methodist missionary among the Blackfeet Indians in southern Alberta in the 1870's, also encountered Tom Faval. His description of Faval matches Schultz's. See John McDougall, *On Western Trails in the Early Seventies* (Toronto, 1911), 150.

my opportunities, I never harmed one, and I don't understand how anyone can trap or shoot them who has had an opportunity to study their habits and mark their wonderful intelligence. In their journal, Lewis and Clark tell of a place they passed on the Missouri where the beavers had cut down four acres of timber. I know a place in the Two Medicine country, where, years ago, the industrious creatures built a dam two-thirds of a mile long and over seven feet in height, thus creating a large artificial lake. The water has long since broken through it, and the beavers have gone. Surely, if there is a hereafter for man, there is for them also.

We left the island at sunrise. There were again many geese here and there on the bars, but they flew long before we came in range of them, and I didn't want one badly enough to go ashore and sneak up on a flock. As we rowed down past the wide Musselshell flat and through the rapids, we saw several flocks of chickens along the shore. Not coveys, but flocks of from twenty-five or thirty up to twice and thrice that number. They band together in large numbers at this season of the year, and it was no uncommon sight to see several hundred of them at morning and evening winging their way across the river. They afford good sport with the shotgun, but neither Sah-né-to nor I care for them; so, except at the beginning of the trip, when we had no meat, we never molested them. Often we passed within a few yards of them, and it was amusing to see them stretch their necks, cock their heads one way and another, and try to make out what we were. From Cow Island down there are also many sagehens in the valley, but strangely enough we never saw any along the shore on the whole trip. Drink they must, but probably not so frequently as do their cousins, the sharptails.

Just east of the Musselshell, on the south side, are a number of very tall buttes, much like the Dark Hills east of the Judith. The formation is the same, brownish-black clays and decayed pumice stone, and many of them are flat-topped and crowned with a heavy stratum of sandstone. Dwarf pines and patches of juniper cling to their barren slopes in places, and between them are deep, dark coulees. No doubt they are the home of many a little band of mule deer, for we saw many tracks of the creatures along the shore until we came to Squaw Creek, four miles below. This is another "dry" stream, coming into the river from the south through a deep, narrow gash in the hills, and here on the north bank of the river opposite it, one of the many tragedies happened for which these badlands are famous. It is quite a story:

In 1862 Nelse Keyser and John Lepley were partners in a placer claim near Helena. Their bar was paying wages, but no more, so it was agreed that Keyser should go prospecting for something better, while his partner worked the claim. A year later he came into Fort Benton from below, and said that he had found some good diggings down the river, showing several hundred dollars' worth of coarse gold dust in evidence of the fact. He went on up to Helena, told his partner his story, and tried to get him to join in working the discovery. But Lepley declined to go, so Keyser sold him his interest in the claim and returned to Fort Benton, where he tried to get several of his friends interested, among them Mr. Jos. Kipp, James Arnoux and George Croff, all living today. But like Lepley, none of them cared to risk their hair down in that hostile Indian country, and beside, they practically had a gold mine in the fur trade. Finally Keyser found a man named Wright to accompany him; they built a large flat boat, loaded it with provisions, mining tools, lumber for sluice boxes, and with their wives—Piegan women—set sail for their Eldorado.

Keyser repeatedly told the women that there were plenty of wild plums in the vicinity of his discovery, and one morning, after they had been on the river some days, he said: "One more sleep and then we will arrive at the place."

At dusk they came to Squaw Creek and went ashore opposite it for the night. They were all sitting around the fire, the women cooking, the men smoking and talking, when suddenly there was an appalling cracking of guns from the surrounding brush, and both of the miners rolled over dead, completely riddled with bullets. Then a party of Assiniboines rushed out, scalped and mutilated their victims, and took the women prisoners, forcing the poor creatures to accompany them to the camp of their people, somewhere out on Milk River. Such of the supplies in the boat as they could not use they set fire to, and turned the craft adrift. It was many months before the captive women finally managed to get away from the camp and tell their story, and although during all these years many prospectors have thoroughly hunted for it, the lost placer has never been found. This much is known: Wild plums grow in the north breaks of the river about a day's drift below Squaw Creek. As Keyser had lumber for sluice boxes, but no horses with which to transport the outfit, his find must have been on, or near, the river. There is no gold-bearing drift in the whole country, so his find must have been a local deposit by the ancient glaciers. Some day it will likely be found, and the lucky man will reap a fortune, for there is no question but what Keyser really struck rich diggings. According to all who knew him, he was a thoroughly reliable and truthful man. His old partner, later a cattle king, and who died only a year ago, staked many a man to look for the claim, so great was his faith that it might be found.*

In the days of Last Chance, Confederate Gulch and the other rich finds of the sixties, there was a constant procession of miners on the road between Helena and Fort Benton on their way back to "the States." Nearly all had some dust, many

*See Granville Stuart, *Forty Years on the Frontier* (Glendale, California, 1967), I, 252–53, for another version of the Keyes (or Keyser) gold mine mystery.

of them small fortunes of the precious metal. Finding no steamboat at the head of navigation, they would start down the river in skiffs and craft of all kinds, regardless of the danger they incurred. New to the country, without experience in the wiles and ways of the Indians, many of these parties were ambushed or shot down as they sat around their campfire. In 1867 one outfit which carried $80,000 in dust, was massacred by the Yanktonais, and they traded the whole sum to a northern half-blood for a couple of kegs of powder and a few sacks of trade balls.

Joseph Kipp, James Arnoux and another whom we will call H., went down the river in a skiff that year. An hour or two before dark they always went ashore and had their evening meal, and then they would go on until absolute darkness overtook them, when they would camp on an island or in the thick brush without a fire, and in that way they got through safely.

I must tell a little incident which happened to the party in Sioux City, for it is typical of the impatience and independence of the men of the plains. They arrived at the small town about noon, and when dinner was announced went into the hotel dining room with the crowd, taking their places at one of the small tables. They were dressed in worn buckskin, were long-haired, unshaven and unkempt, and the negro waiters seemed to think that the more respectably dressed guests should be served first. So there they sat and sat, toying with their knives and forks, and saw the other guests helped to meat, to all there was, and finally to pie. H. had repeatedly beckoned to a waiter who had charge of the next table, and presumably of the one they were at also, and each time he had replied, "Yes, sah. In just a minute, sah," but he never came near them.

When H. saw the others helped to pie and finishing their meal, that was more than he could stand. Rising and following the waiter into the kitchen, he drew and cocked both of his guns, and said, "Now, then, you black rascal, wait on us quick or I'll fill your old carcass with lead. Fill one of those trays with all kinds of grub you've got and a pie for each of us, and rustle out with it. A pie apiece, mind you, and be quick." The trembling negro hastened to do as he was told, while the cook and others vacated the place by windows and doors. Probably that waiter filled the order quicker than one ever was filled anywhere before or since, and H. kept right at his back until the food was placed on the table. But even then they were not destined to appease their appetites, for they had not near got to the pie before the proprietor of the hotel, the town marshal, a sheriff and three constables came in and arrested H. for flourishing deadly weapons with intent to kill, and the others for aiding and abetting him. As Mr. Kipp expressed it, this "was duck soup for the administrators of justice and the shyster lawyers." It cost the party $450 and two days' time to settle the matter. H. says that his only regret was that he didn't get to eat the pie. He hadn't seen any for ten years, and wanted it bad.

Just below Squaw Creek, on the same side, begins a remarkably picturesque series of pine-crowned sandstone bluffs, which form the rim of the valley for a distance of eight or ten miles. When we arrived at Hornet Island, which is opposite the center of their length, we went ashore to look around a bit. This is no longer an island, except during the spring raise, the whole river having shifted to the north side, leaving a broad sandbar between it and the south shore. There was a large pool of water in the bar, however, about opposite the center of the island, and, as I expected, we found its margin all tracked up by both kinds of deer. There were also the more forked and stubby tracks of mountain sheep which had come down the bluffs to quench their thirst.

Well aware that our forequarters of the deer were about

gone, at least such portions of it as we cared to eat, I proposed to replenish our larder here, and suggested to Sah-né-to that it might be a good plan for her to drive the island. She objected, on the ground that there were likely two or three grizzlies lurking in its timbered recesses. We went down then the whole length of the bar, and having convinced her that no beast of prey larger than a coyote had crossed it, she concluded it was safe enough, and entered the willows and timber. I hurried back to the upper end of the island and posted myself in the brush on the main shore near a well-beaten trail crossing the bar. Five, ten minutes passed, and then a red fox came off of the island and trotted directly toward me, stopping now and then to look back and listen. When he was within twenty feet of me I leaned out and said "Boo!" and how he did make the sand fly as he scurried for shelter. I could now hear Sah-né-to shouting occasionally, and presently five deer burst out of the opposite brush and came spread out over the same trail the fox had. They also passed within twenty feet of the brush I was in, but never saw me. After a little Sah-né-to appeared.

"Why didn't you shoot him?" she asked.

"I didn't see any 'him,'" I replied; "they were all does and fawns."

"Well," she continued, "there was also a buck. I saw him plainly, and he had a very large set of antlers."

We tried for an hour to get a shot at the old fellow, but he was too cute for us, circling back in the thick willows every time. Maybe he had had some experience before in fleeing from the sound of a voice across an open sandbar. So we pushed out into the stream, and no doubt when he saw us passing he kicked up his heels and wiggled his tail and laid down for another snooze.

We had been running north all the morning, making the balance of the twenty miles around the point opposite the

Musselshell. At Hornet Island the river turns eastward again, and a favorable wind having sprung up, we hoisted the sail and pulled in the oars. The next bend below the island on the north side is called Horseshoe Point, and is about a mile square. As we rounded the outer end of it there were two whitetail out on the shore, and the minute they saw us, back they went into the timber. We ran ashore and found the sandbar all cut up by deer tracks, and taking the rifle, I slowly climbed the bank and walked back a short distance toward the bluffs. Not far, however, as the thick rose brush was almost impenetrable, and extended several feet above my head. Mounting a fallen log, I got a good view of the bottom. Except for a narrow belt of green timber fringing the shore, the whole flat was a tangle of burned and fallen trees, and grown up with the thickest, tallest rose brush I ever saw. No doubt it harbored many deer, but I didn't want one of them bad enough to venture into the thickets. Mornings and evenings, standing quietly anywhere in the edge of the green belt, or back on the slope of the hills, one could not fail to get a piece of meat.

Two miles below the point are Striped Bluff Rapids, so named from the peculiarly stratified cut wall along the south side of them. They are narrow and deep, and not particularly swift. After passing over them we went on about three miles further, and stopped on Elk Island for lunch. It is well timbered, nearly a mile long, and the old channel between it and the north shore has filled with sand. It was too large to be driven by one person, so we did not attempt it. There were a number of deer on it, as evidenced by their numerous tracks in the sand. I have seen other game here. Going down to Bismarck once, on the steamer *Helena*, we ran into a large herd of buffalo opposite the island. Several of us who were standing on the low bow of the boat, made some nooses of the ropes piled there, and tried to slip them over the heads of some of the animals we were running down. The hawsers were so heavy, however, that we couldn't handle them, and very likely if we had succeeded in roping one we would have had plenty of trouble on our hands, and the rope to pay for.

The animals tried their best to keep out of the way, plunging and swimming frantically, but the flat-bottomed boat ran over a number without injuring them, apparently. I have often wondered why the buffalo would persist in crossing and recrossing this great river, when range and feed was as good on one side as on the other. And generally they seemed to select the worst places for doing so, milling around and around under high cut banks until they drowned, or attempting to cross a quicksand only to mire down. In old times, in the days of Lewis and Clark, for instance, more of them must have annually died in this manner than from the arrows of all the tribes on the river.

I told Sah-né-to about trying to rope buffalo here from the bow of a steamboat, and the incident reminded her of an experience of her brother with the animals somewhere on the river. With four others he started to raid the horse herds of the Yanktonais Sioux. The party was very small, and believing they were less likely to be discovered, they concluded to travel on the south side of the river until they passed the Musselshell. Night after night they kept traveling eastward, each morning repairing to the timbered breaks and building a "war house" wherein to sleep and cook. After passing the Musselshell the partisan of the party, the leader and carrier of the "medicine," had a bad dream: "I can't say what is going to happen," he told the others, "but the medicine has warned me that there is danger ahead. Let us be extra cautious."

That day, counciling together, they decided that it was time to recross the river, for they were now in the Yanktonais country and liable to run across a camp of them at any time. So, late in the afternoon, they cautiously descended into a timbered bottom and began to construct a small raft on which to pile their clothing and weapons. It was in early summer, and the river was very high and running swiftly. They were some little time collecting the material, and the sun was just setting when they pushed out into the stream, each one holding to the raft and kicking with all his might to propel it toward the other shore.

The swift current, however, was sweeping into the south shore, and in spite of their best endeavors they could not force the raft across it, so there was no alternative but to drift along and wait until it should carry them to the opposite side. Down around the bend they went, and suddenly found themselves bearing into a herd of buffalo swimming the river. They were so close that it was too late to forsake the raft and attempt to swim ashore, for they were now out in midstream. All four of them swung around to the south side of the raft and bore down on it, raising the opposite side as much as they could as a sort of barrier.

In among the swimming animals they floated, such a dense mass of them that the water could hardly be seen. The frail logs bumped and rubbed against them, but they scarcely deviated from their course; they could not, so closely were they crowding each other. Those coming on toward the raft also struck it, and tried to paw and climb upon it, snorting and blowing, and others behind crowding on caused great confusion, the stronger ones thrusting the smaller under the surface, and once in a while one of these would bob up under the men, who could only kick and shout, and splash the water in their endeavors to frighten the animals away.

The buffalo were as scared as the men, and more than one of them lunged at the raftsmen viciously, and several times nearly impaled one on their sharp horns. The continual bumping and crowding of the animals against the logs kept forcing the raft back toward the south shore, and after a little it grounded on a bar. Then the Indians stood behind it and picking up some of their clothing, shirts or leggins, swung them frantically, and the buffalo, striking the shallow water, rushed by on either side, giving them as wide a berth as possible. In a little while all had passed, and then the party once more shoved out and reached the other shore without further trouble.

"See now," the partisan said, "how faithful our medicine; it warned us of this danger we have just passed through. I believe it is a good omen; we will be successful."

And they were. A few days later they stampeded over a hundred head of the enemy's horses and brought them safely home.

IX

FIVE miles below Elk Island is Devils, or Rattlesnake Creek. It cuts through a flat thirty feet or more above the river, and its slopes are covered with massive, irregular blocks of the soft badlands soil which the water has undermined. In among these blocks are many crevices and miniature caves, no doubt much frequented by snakes. The cottontail rabbits also make their homes in such places, and as they are nowhere especially numerous along the river, I believe that their numbers are kept down by the rattlers.

Two miles further down we came to the mouth of the Fourchette, a running stream which heads forty or fifty miles away to the north, near the Little Rockies. It enters the Missouri through a wide, sloping valley, and has a fringe of cottonwoods and willows along its course. This point was always a favorite camping place with the Indians in other days, as the buffalo and elk seemed to frequent the vicinity the year around. In the winter of 1862–63 Major George Stull managed a small post here for the American Fur Company, and did a large trade with the Gros Ventres and Assiniboines. That was the winter Nelse Keyser found his placer mine, and the Major says that he came to the post several times during the season for supplies. He never told exactly where he was located, but pointing away to the southwest would say: "There is my country. There's where I am going to make a big stake."*

---

*John Largent wrote in Robert Vaughn, *Then and Now, Thirty-Six Years in the Rockies* (Minneapolis, 1900), 181, that he was employed by Major George "Steell" in the construction and operation of Fort Andrews at the mouth of the Musselshell River. Largent stated that a "Nelse Kies" worked a gold mine downriver from the mouth of the Musselshell. Kies visited the post at least once, but was killed by the

One time during that winter a large party of Crows came into the post, ostensibly to trade some robes and furs. The trade room was a long, low cabin, and across it ran a counter nearly five feet high, behind which the goods were piled on shelves. The room was packed full of the Indians, and while the Major was trading with one of them, the others began to climb up on the counter and reach over for one thing and another. "When he gets mad," he heard one of them say, "everyone shoot and then we'll clean the place out quick."

The next instant they saw two six-shooters pointed at them, and the Major said: "I'll kill the first man who starts to raise his gun or bow. Get out of this room at once, every one of you. Hurry, for these guns are going to begin talking very soon."

The Crows stood for a little in astonishment, and then a panic seized them and they rushed for the door, pulling, pushing and trampling on each other in their hurry, dropping and leaving their bundles of robes and skins. About that time the cook and a couple of half-blood employees came over from the other cabin, and then the Major went to the door and faced the crowd, who were now protesting that they meant no harm, and begging for their property. He told them that five of their number could come in and trade at a time, and they did so. But the first in traded some robes belonging to others, and afterward there was a big row, in which three men were killed.

Passing around Trover Point, long and narrow, we came to the mouth of Killed Woman Creek, a "dry" stream also coming in from the north. Years ago a camp of Assiniboines were attacked here by a war party of Teton and Ogallalla Sioux, and one woman was killed, hence the name of the stream. It is not generally known, I believe, that these branches of the

---

Indians before he revealed the exact location of his gold diggings, according to Largent.

great Sioux nation warred upon each other, but such was the case. The Assiniboine Sioux separated from the others nearly two hundred years ago, after a quarrel over some women, and came west. They never increased, as their numbers were kept down by the new enemies they found, principally the Black-feet.

Opposite the mouth of the little creek we saw a skiff tied to a stake, and going ashore beside it, I climbed the trail leading to the top of the high bank. Just as I reached the top I nearly ran into a man coming after a bucket of water, and was not a little surprised to recognize my old friend Ed. Herman. "Well, well," he exclaimed, almost yanking me off my feet. "What on earth are you doing down here?"

"Oh," I replied, "just drifting along and revisiting our old stamping grounds with Sah-né-to. And you?"

"Why, I'm building here and am going to buy a few cattle. There's my shack over there; just bring up your bedding and things and make yourselves comfortable until next spring at least."

The first news that Ed. had to tell was that no whitetail deer has died below the mouth of the Fourchette of the disease which had so decimated their numbers further up the river. "I'm thinking of going into the sheep business also," he continued. "Just come out here a minute."

I went with him to a ridge a couple of hundred yards back of the cabin, which extended from the breaks down across the bottom to the river. Along its crest was a well-worn trail. "Just look at those tracks in the dust and tell me what made them," he said.

"Why, bighorn," I exclaimed. "There have been a lot of them along here recently, and from the looks of the tracks some of them were big rams."

"Exactly. They come down here for water every night, but I have never seen them on their way to or from the river. They are too wise to make the trip in the daytime. Whenever I go up in the breaks, however, I always see one or more bunches of them."

The country back of Herman's ranch is an ideal place for sheep, as it is a tangled network of deep coulees and high ridges, of rocky buttes and rough cliffs. Some of these deep coulees extend southward toward the Yellowstone for twenty miles. The bighorn in these badlands rut in October, and bring forth their young in March, two months earlier in each case than the bighorn of the Rockies, only two to three hundred miles away. The difference in the altitude is the reason for this. The trees along the Missouri are in leaf before the snow disappears from the mountain slopes. Herman said that he saw rams with the ewes the latter part of September. On a recent ramble back in the breaks he had found the remains of a yearling ram killed by a mountain lion, and said that he frequently saw tracks of the big cats along the river bars.

We stopped with Ed. overnight, and were early afloat. At the lower end of his flat the river enters a narrow canyon, and the strips of bottom land are barren except for the ever-present growth of sage. Here and there a few cottonwoods and willows grow near the water's edge, but there is not enough timber to shelter the brush-loving whitetail deer for a distance of thirty miles, where, at the Round Butte, the valley widens out again and the bottoms support large groves of cottonwoods. Yet this thirty-mile stretch is one of the most picturesque parts of the river. From Herman's ranch to the mouth of Seven Blackfeet Creek, the southern rim of the valley is one continuous cliff of sandstone, pierced by walled coulees, capped with a lovely fringe of green timber. And on the slopes, below the frowning walls, stretches the heaviest growth of pines and firs of any we had seen. An ideal mule deer country, I thought, and the numerous tracks of the animals along the bars proved that I was right. At the mouth of the Seven Blackfeet we found a small clump of cottonwoods, enough to shelter a tent and furnish a little fuel, and after scraping over a wide, shallow bar, we managed to make a landing within a few yards of them. We put up the tent on a bit of grass land under the trees and got everything in shape for the night, as I had determined to spend the day prowling around in the breaks.

On the state map this little stream is marked Quarrel Creek, but its right name is as I have given it. Years ago a party of seven of the Piegan branch of the Blackfeet were crossing the flat here one day, on their way to raid the camp of the Yanktonais, further down the river. As luck would have it, a very large party of the Sioux, traveling up the river, saw them, and waiting until they were on the barren flat, charged down out of the breaks and hemmed them in. There was nothing behind which the besieged party could shelter themselves; they had no time to dig pits with their knives. They realized, no doubt, that their time had come, but they met the end bravely, shooting at the enemy with careful aim, singing the war song with spirit, falling one by one on the barren plain until all were dead, when the Sioux rushed in and took their scalps, their weapons and war finery. Five of the Sioux also fell during the brief battle, and three more were wounded.

The Seven Blackfeet is not much of a stream, although it is nearly forty miles in length, rising far to the south in the rough country toward the Yellowstone. The bottom through which it flows into the Missouri is nearly four miles long, but less than a mile wide, and is covered with a dense growth of high sagebrush. The previous winter, riding by on the opposite side of the river, Herman and a friend of his had counted a band of sixty-three bighorn on the flat, all grown animals, the kids being invisible in the tall sage. There were many fresh signs of them along the shore where we camped, as well as plenty of mule deer tracks, and when I started out for the breaks after an early lunch, I felt sure that I would see some of them. Crossing the flat I began to climb the sloping point on the right, or west side of the creek. For the most part the soil was barren, and after the last rain it had dried hard on the surface, so that one could almost imagine he was walking on crusted snow, it crunched with a sound exactly like it.

Part way up the ridge a band of mule deer which had been lying in a patch of junipers got wind of me, and disappeared into a deep coulee before I could get a shot. When I next saw them they were a quarter of a mile away on the opposite side of the creek. I kept on up the hill without stopping until I reached the crest, and found myself on a long backbone or ridge running parallel with the river. Deep-timbered coulees, cut cliffs, were the general features upon each side of it, and not far westward of where I stood, rising above the level of the ridge, stood a massive block of sandstone, aptly named from its shape the Cabin Butte. Its sides are nearly rectangular walls, and its top is shaped like an ordinary roof. All around the base of the great rock I found many tracks of bighorn, old and fresh, and their beds, shallowly scooped in the sandy earth. One gets a fine view from here both of the Missouri and the valley of the Seven Blackfeet, walled with sandstone cliffs. Thousands of coulees run into it; away toward its headwaters odd-shaped buttes, some pine-covered, loom up above the general level of the plain. And away to the southwest can be seen the Bull Mountains, as we used to call them, but which are marked Piney Buttes on recent maps.

After resting and enjoying a smoke, I descended the south side of the ridge and kept on through a rough lot of hills and cliffs for a mile or more, scaring up two small bands of bighorn, and one bunch of mule deer. Then I crossed the creek valley and began to work toward camp through the heads of the coulees and the hills on that side. The first thing I ran across here was a bear track several days old, but a sure proof that bruin was somewhere around in the breaks. I had got into an exceedingly rough bit of country, cut walls and nearly perpendicular-sided coulees, when I ran across a bunch of five mule deer, one of them a goodly buck. They rose up out of some stunted pines and stood staring at me, and I raised the rifle, when I suddenly realized that if I killed the buck I would have a difficult task to get him out of the breaks and over the four miles to camp. So I didn't shoot, but slung my hat at them instead and enjoyed seeing them stilt away up the coulee. Mule deer are certainly ungraceful jumpers.

From there on to camp I saw nothing of any kind of game except numerous tracks, much to my surprise, and then I regretted not having shot the buck back in the breaks, for we were out of meat. Yet, when I raised the tent flaps I met a savory odor of something roasting in the stove oven, and upon sitting down to the spread of good things which was ready, found that Sah-né-to had been on a little hunt herself; the result, two fat cottontails nicely dressed, broken down flat and roasted with a few crisp slices of breakfast bacon on top of the brown, tender meat. She said that while I was away in the hills three deer had come down to water on the opposite side of the river, and then gone back into the breaks.

After dinner was over it still lacked an hour to sunset, so Sah-né-to and I strolled down along the shore for about a mile, to a small dry island, which has a few scattering trees upon it. The shores and sandbar thereabouts were all cut up with trails and tracks of sheep and deer, and I felt sure we would soon see some game of some kind. We sat down in a patch of short willows and I gave Sah-né-to the rifle, telling her it was her turn to kill a deer. She had fired one shot only once before, and protested that she would be sure to miss. The time referred to, a coyote had come nosing around our house when she happened to be there alone, and she had mustered up courage to take a shot at it, whereupon the ani-

mal had run away down the creek at top speed. A week later
we found a dead coyote about half a mile from the ranch.
"There," she exclaimed, "that must be my coyote; it looks
exactly like the one I shot at."

We told her that all coyotes looked alike, but upon examin-
ing the carcass found a bullet hole clear through it, and concluded that she had killed it.

We sat quietly in the willows for half an hour or more, and
then a lone doe mule deer appeared on the bank. We could
see only her head and brisket as she looked up and down,
and back whence she came. After a little, satisfied that everything was as it should be, she came out of the sagebrush and
started down the bank to the water, and then we saw that
there were others—nine, in fact, all does and fawns. Sah-né-to
was excited. "Which one will I shoot?" she asked, raising and
cocking the rifle. "None," I replied. "Don't you see that there
is no buck among them?"

"Yes, but also I know there is no meat in camp. I will try to
hit that nearest fawn."

It was all I could do to keep her from shooting. The deer
went to the river's edge just above the island, drank their
fill, nosed around and slowly reclimbed the bank, fading away
into the sagebrush as stealthily as they had come. Then I read
Sah-né-to a short lecture on game preservation. "The does,"
I said, "should not be killed unless a person absolutely needs
the meat. If we were starving, it would be different. There are
plenty of deer here along the river, and no doubt we will get
a buck this evening or tomorrow."

We saw none, however, although we remained on the island until dusk, and then returned to camp. The night was
chilly, and a good fire in the stove made the tent very comfortable. Away down the river we heard the honk, honk of
an approaching flock of geese, and then their soft, satisfied
guttural murmuring as they lit on the bar not far below. A

couple of owls in the nearby trees asked each other "Who? Who?" and then somewhere out on the flat a band of wolves serenaded us. Is there anything more melancholy than their deep and long-drawn cry? One can well imagine that they are mourning for the days that are gone—days of the buffalo and a plenty of all the wild things which were their prey. If so, they are not alone. There are others—white men as well as Indians—who would gladly see the towns and the ranches and the railroads swept from the face of the earth, if they could once more roam these plains, as they were before all such things came to be. No luxuries of modern civilized life can make up for the simple contentment of those other times.

"Listen," said Sah-né-to. "What causes that splashing in the river?"

We went outside, and in the dim moonlight could see a commotion out in the middle of the stream, a splashing and rippling of the water, but not the object which caused it. "Oh," I remarked, "it's probably a beaver, or maybe an otter playing with its young. Let's go back inside; it is cold out here."

Sah-né-to stirred the fire and put a fresh stick in the stove. "Yes," she said, thoughtfully, "it might have been a beaver or an otter, as you say, but it seems to me that there was more splashing and noise in the water than either of those animals could have made. I believe it was a *su-yi-top-pi* (literally, under-water person). This is the time, a moonlight night, when they come to the surface and play around."

"What are they like?" I asked. "Did any of your people ever see one?"

"Indeed they did," she replied. "Long ago the camp was pitched on that stream in the north we call the Elk River. One day a man sitting on the edge of a high cut bank happening to look down in the great clear pool below, saw a strange-looking object moving around in the depths. He could not see it clearly, it was so far beneath the surface, but he thought it must be one of the *su-yi-top-pi*, and he hastened to call the people. When they arrived, and cautiously peered over the edge of the bank, it had come up quite near the surface, and was resting on its back, its arms crossed behind its head. It was a man, far taller than any man who walks on the land, and quite slender in proportion to its height. It had a white skin, and its long, light hair, eddying and waving in the water, completely veiled its face, so that no one saw it. For a little time, while the people gazed at it in fear and wonder, it rested nearly motionless, and then slowly making a couple of strokes with its hands, sank down and down, and disappeared in the blue depths.

"There were more of them here in this river than any other one, but after the steamboats began to run they became scarce. The old men say that the great wheels of the boats struck and killed many of them. Once somewhere on this river, I think it was below the Great Roar (Great Falls), a party in search of berries saw a woman sitting on a big rock out in the stream. She also had wonderfully long and thick light-colored hair, which fell over and covered her face completely, and through which could be seen only here and there the white gleam of her breasts. Seeing the people coming along the shore, she quickly slid off the rock and sank out of sight.

"The wise men say that the *su-yi-top-pi* do not eat persons, for the bodies of the unfortunates they drag down to their death are generally found without a bruise or mark of any kind. Otters, fish and hell divers constitute their food; and also the mussels. One time when the people were traveling south to hunt in the Yellow Creek country, they came to the ford on the Missouri right where the wagon bridge at Great Falls now stands. As they approached the bank they saw a number of otters hastening downstream over the ford, and one very large one, which seemed to be the leader, kept throwing himself out of the water and making a queer noise, as if urging the others on. They all seemed to be scared at something. Now, when the chiefs and the medicine men and some of the great warriors, who were in the lead, rode to the shore, their horses instead of walking into the water, stopped and snorted, and backed up, trying to turn and run. Then every one knew that some *su-yi-top-pi* were out there in the river, and that they had scared the otters. So the people went into camp right there, not daring to attempt the ford. The next day, however, the horses showed no fear of the river, and the camp crossed over and went on."

"Well," I asked, after a little, "is that all you have to tell me about them?"

"That is all for tonight. Tomorrow I will make them a sacrifice, for we seem to be getting into their country."

X

WE were now in the wildest part of the upper Missouri Valley, a country so interesting, of such vast extent of canyon-like ravines, of cliffs and buttes and weird, weather-carved sandstones, that I would have liked to pitch camp every four of five miles or so along down the river and explore all the interesting places. But the lateness of the season prevented. The river had frozen over the previous year on November 10; it nearly always freezes some time during that month, and the middle of the month had been passed. With regret we broke camp at the mouth of the Seven Blackfeet and resumed our voyage just as the sun appeared above the breaks to the east.

The channel here is on the north side of the river, and I had some difficulty in getting the Good Shield over the rocky bar out into deep water. At this point the river bends sharply to the north around a long, high broken ridge, a most likely lurking place for mountain sheep. On the south side of the stream, high up in the breaks, there are scattering groves of pine, but the slopes are of barren blue clay, which wash away so rapidly under the influence of the rain and melting snow, that it is impossible for any kind of vegetation to flourish. A row of three miles took us to the Buffalo Shoals, a wide, rapid, shallow bit of the river. I told Sah-né-to the name of the place, and, of course, she had something to say about the great herds which used to ford here. But her remarks were cut short by the jar of the boat as it bumped over some rocks and came to a dead stop.

I stood up and tried to make out the channel, but here was one place where there was nothing to indicate it; from bank to bank nothing but an undulating ripple of the water over the stones. I put on my waders and holding the boat firmly by the bow, dragged it back upstream a short distance, and slowly began to cross to the north side, until I found two feet of water, and then waded slowly down behind the craft, letting it float ahead of me. It ran aground several times, and I found that what channel there was wound like the letter S across the shoal.

We had no more than floated into the deep water below it when Sah-né-to espied an animal of some kind hurrying across the flat below toward the river. On it came, trotting rapidly, down on to the sandy bar and buried its nose in the water. Then we saw that it was a buck mule deer, and a very large one. I dared not row, for fear of alarming it, and picking up the rifle waited for the boat to drift down within range. But the buck was in a hurry; he had important business somewhere back in the hills, and having satisfied his thirst, trotted away as fast as he had come, while we were yet five hundred yards distant. "Go," I said, "and good luck to you; I think there are fatter bucks than you to be found."

All the same, I was disappointed; it would have been so handy to kill the meat we needed right on the shore. We kept on running northward for three or four miles, and then the river bent to the east again past long, narrow, almost treeless flats, and by rough hills and cliffs. After something like eleven or twelve miles of hard rowing we came to a nameless creek, putting in from the south through tall and fantastic portals of sandstone. On the west side of it, on top of a high ridge, stands a peculiar sandstone formation, which the United States engineers who surveyed the river named the Sphinx, and, viewed from a point on the river anywhere east of the nameless creek, it certainly does bear a striking resemblance to that old monument of ancient Egypt.

Looking at this and at the surrounding hills, the walled valley of the creek, I felt that I could not forego a ramble in such an interesting place. A mile or more below there was a wooded island, from which a sandy bar extended to the south shore; the channel ran in to its outer side, and we landed only a few yards from the grove. The trees were scattering, the underbrush was interspersed with plots of tall grass that bore the impression of many a deer bed. In one of these open places the tent was pitched and a few blows of the ax on a large dead cottonwood brought down sheets of thick bark, sufficient for several days' fuel. That is one of the advantages of camping along this river; it is not necessary to do any chopping. One can quietly row to a cottonwood grove, pitch camp, secure fuel without disturbing the game in the immediate vicinity. The loose dry cottonwood bark can be pried from the trunk and noiselessly broken into convenient size for the stove.

While I was eating a bit of lunch, Sah-né-to strolled out on the wide sandy bar at the head of the island, and quickly returned with the information that she had seen a bear track. So, without any questioning, I knew that I was to have company on my ramble. Where the rifle is there will always be the madame when bears are around; not for all the wealth of the country would she remain alone in camp after seeing the trail of one, for it was well known that they had even "carried women away to their dens and made slaves of them."

We started, crossing the long sand spit connecting the island with the main shore, and thence up the hard mud margin of the river to the mouth of the nameless creek. Here were tracks of game galore; of mountain sheep and mule deer, of wolf and coyote, and of the grizzly, which had been recently prowling along the shore in search of a dead fish or other morsel of food cast up by the eddying waters. We climbed the steep bank, twenty or thirty feet high, and stood on the edge of the long flat among the giant sage and greasewood, some of which was taller than our heads.

Away up the creek was a bunch of horses. When they saw us they lifted their heads and gazed at us curiously for a moment, and then bounded away up the narrow valley as fast as they could go, startling a little bunch of antelope, which also scurried off across the flat and up into the breaks. Perhaps they were wild horses—horses which had never felt the touch of a lariat, nor the burning sizzling brand. Here, if any place, in this vast extent of badlands lying between the Missouri and the Yellowstone, there should still be some of these untamed descendants of the Spanish conquistadors' steeds.

Once, traveling with Mr. Joseph Kipp from our trading post on the Missouri to the branch post on the Flat Willow, we saw a band of these wild horses. I think it was in the fall of 1880. We had crossed Crooked Creek, and climbing to the top of a high pine-crowned butte, stopped to rest our horses and survey the country. War parties, we knew, were abroad— Sioux, Assiniboines, Crows and Cheyennes—and we didn't intend to run into any of them if we could help it. It was a broken bit of country we surveyed. Tall buttes, long ridges, deep coulees on either hand, with glimpses of the dead grass and sagebrush plain stretching away for untold miles to the verge of the horizon. Away to the north of us, across, beyond the dark breaks of the Missouri, loomed the Little Rockies and their terminating pine-clad butte, the Hairy Cap. West of them we could see the flat tops of the Bear Paws. To the south, near at hand, was the Black Butte, a dark, high, steep cone of volcanic rock, and still further on, the green slopes and bare peaks of the Snowy Range.

As we sat there, smoking and viewing this great expanse of plains and mountains, and rough country, a herd of wild horses, a hundred or more, came dashing down the valley of Crooked Creek, climbed the ridge near us, and swept on toward the Musselshell. Some were bays, some blacks, with no inconsiderable number of gray and dun-colored ones.

Their exceedingly long and full manes and tails streamed out in the breeze. They were sleek-coated and fat, and by the way they arched their necks and pranced along they seemed to have a grand and invincible spirit, which I for one would not have cared to attempt to conquer. Some wolves, disturbed in their slumber, perhaps by the thunder of the horses' hoofs, trotted to the edge of the butte opposite us, and looked at them longingly, hungrily; they prefer the flesh of the horse, it seems, above any other meat. Only a few moments after the band had passed us, a large herd of buffalo came in sight from the same direction that they had. "There are no camps of hunting Indians near here," my companion remarked, "so these herds must have been scared by a war party. Let's go."

We went. On and on, past groups of buttes and high ridges, over stretches of level plain, by many a herd of buffalo and antelope, and far in the night arrived at our destination, tired and hungry. We had no thought that all that game we saw was soon to vanish, and that the wide plains we crossed were soon to be dotted with vast herds of the accursed sheep.

Well, the horses and the antelope vanished. Antelope are protected the year round in Montana, nevertheless if I could have got within range of one of the bucks I would have killed him. I believe in the protection of game. I will not kill a female, deer nor elk, nor any other species. But when I'm out of meat, the first buck of any kind I run across has got to fall if I can aim straight enough. If all hunters would forego the shooting of females, we would have no need for game protection. For instance, three years ago a friend of mine killed three does. There was no excuse for his doing so, as we had the meat of a good buck in camp. Now, if those three had lived, they and their increase would have numbered about fourteen head this coming spring.

We crossed the flat, passing through a prairie dog town, where the little animals were so tame that they sat up on their mounds within fifteen or twenty yards of us, and scolded us unmercifully. Evidently they knew nothing about men and rifles. We left them, still barking and jerking their tails, and began the ascent of the valley slope west of the little creek. The barren, blue clay hill, as usual, had a hard rasping crust, which afforded good walking. We climbed up easily, through a grove of scattering pine, past clumps of juniper, and coming to the foot of the Sphinx, were surprised to find that it rests on the edge of a high, long, cut sandstone wall. All along its base there were many bighorn tracks, and nearby lay the skull and horns of a large ram. From the Sphinx southward to the next ridge, a distance of perhaps two miles, there has been a sudden sinking of the country, resulting in a rough grassy plain seamed with cracks, which would be difficult to cross. I had intended to go that way, but concluded to go back down and across the nameless creek, and hunt the opposite side.

We were resting at the foot of the Sphinx and viewing the rough country to the west, tall steep buttes and cut cliffs, when, about a quarter of a mile away a large ram appeared at the foot of the cliff we were sitting on, evidently following the trail of some of its kind. He would trot a ways, always with his nose close to the ground, and often stop and circle a bit, and look around, as if having lost the scent. When we first saw him, he was coming toward us, but while still a long ways off, he began to climb the cliff on a place where it seemed as if it would be impossible to sustain a foothold. Up he went, however, rapidly, and with apparent ease, and disappeared in some pines. I thought of following him, and, indeed, we traveled along three or four hundred yards in the direction he had taken, and then we saw a bunch of the animals bounding up the side of a butte some distance ahead. They paused on attaining the summit—there were between fifteen and twenty of them—looked at us a moment or two, and then ran on out of sight, their white stern ends bobbing up and down most ludicrously. Well, I reasoned that it was nearly if not quite past the rutting season, that a ram's meat would be unpleasantly rank, so I bade Sah-né-to turn, and we retraced our way past the Sphinx and followed the ridge down into the valley.

On the east side of the little creek are many thickets and groves of pine, dense beds of juniper brush, most likely places, I thought, for a mule deer's siesta. We climbed up through several of them, finding plenty of sign, deer tracks and beds, and presently an exceedingly large old buck slowly arose from a patch of brush on a ridge across a narrow coulee from us, and calmly stood gazing our way most inquisitively. I cocked the rifle and handed it to Sah-né-to, and she hurriedly aimed and fired. The old buck made one jump up the hill and looked at us as before. Twice more Sah-né-to fired before the old fellow ran, and then he stopped before he had gone more than fifty yards and gave her another chance. But that was the last one; unhurt, untouched, he bounded stiffly up the ridge and over the crest of the hill. "Did you look carefully through the little hole in the rear sight, and get the ivory bead fairly on him?" I asked.

"I don't know. I guess not," she replied. "I just kept looking at him and shooting."

That was what I had already guessed; she had been too excited to think of the sights.

We continued our climb until we arrived at the foot of a steep wall, where we found a broad and hard-beaten game trail running along its base, used principally by mountain sheep. Sah-né-to was becoming tired, so we climbed no higher, and followed the trail in the direction of the river and camp. Numberless deep coulees headed up against the cliff, and we kept descending and ascending them, until we finally came into one that extended back to the east further than we could see. Here the game trail branched, the main one crossing the coulee, the lesser one continuing along the foot of the cliff, which, like the ravine, now bore away to the east, forming its southern wall. It was this one we followed, and after a while came into a sort of amphitheater, caused by the junction of a number of smaller coulees.

Here on all sides, in every conceivable shape, domes, columns, and all sorts of queer-shaped figures, was the blue clay, devoid of any vegetation whatever, nor could we see a living thing—no tree nor brush in any direction. Inadvertently stepping into the bottom of the coulee, I went down into a soft alkali mud, but scrambled out of it before I pierced its depth; perhaps it had no end. I sat down, and with a bit of rock was cleaning my leggins and shoes, when with a clatter and rush a band of sheep slipped out of a coulee back of us and in an instant were out of sight over the trail we had been following. We did not follow them.

This was about as barren a bit of nature as I had ever seen. One could imagine that in the course of his work the hand of the world maker had been stopped and his plan had remained uncompleted. I expressed something of my thought to Sah-né-to, and she said that Old Man had himself finished these plains, and caused the grasses to grow upon them, but afterward he cut the gash where the Big River should run and from that cut the rains had kept wearing away the banks on either side, forming the deep coulees and hills, and carrying off the top soil which alone could support vegetation.

We went up the coulee a ways further, climbed a steep ridge and got on top of a long, narrow point overlooking another coulee. All the morning during our ramble we had seen numerous deposits of red iron rock, but here we found large quantities of it, always in flat, circular form, as if it had been melted in a furnace and moulded in this shape. I lifted one or two of the smaller cakes and found them very heavy. They were scattered promiscuously here and there on top of the clay. Crossing the next coulee, and over the next ridge we found that we were abreast our camp only a half-mile away across the flat, and as by this time Sah-né-to was tired out, we turned homeward, seeing no more game, although there were fresh tracks everywhere.

As we descended into the flat a dense low bank of dark fog rolled in from the north down the opposite slope, and a few minutes later a fierce cold wind was howling over the plains, and it became so dark that we could not see our island. The sudden change chilled us thoroughly, and by the time we arrived at the tent our fingers and ears were tingling. In two or three minutes I had the stove red hot, the tent sufficiently warm, and Sah-né-to began preparations for dinner. I have tried all sorts of temporary camps, from the bark shelters of the Adirondacks to the skin lodge of the plains, but have found nothing to equal the tent and stove for comfort.

It had been another unsuccessful day, although in a section of country abounding in game, the camp was still bare of the juicy roasts, broils and rib stews necessary for our complete contentment. "Sah-né-to, 'twas your fault; if you had taken careful aim at the buck, his carcass would now hang on the tree just beyond the doorway."

"It is done," she replied. "The cartridges have been fired, the deer has bounded away into the hills; let us talk no more about it."

Thinking over the incidents of the day, of the ram so accurately trailing a band of his kind, reminded me of a young elk I used to see on Upper Arrow Creek. Some Indians had caught it when it was a calf and given it to Mrs. La Mott, whose husband kept a roadhouse. She raised it, feeding it milk at first from a bottle, and gradually teaching it to drink from a pan, and it became so attached to her that it would bleat most dismally whenever separated from her for a few moments. Sometimes to tease it Mrs. La Mott would put it outside by the front door and then leaving the house at the rear side run to the timber bordering the creek, and thence up the stream, crossing it several times, and finally make a circuit around back to the stables. It was never many minutes before the uneasy calf, strolling around to the back of the house, found her footsteps, and trailed her accurately around the course she had taken. Often balked where her mistress had jumped a creek or crossed on stepping stones, it would circle about until it found the trail once more, and hasten on with all speed, and how it would jump and buck and play around when it finally overtook her.

The little thing was hated by the "mule skinners." The freight outfits were obliged to camp at Arrow Creek on account of water, and it was amusing to see the weary, dusty, thirsty mules take after the young elk as soon as they were unharnessed. The calf would start up the road at first on a walk, the mules crowding after it, all curiosity, crowding and kicking each other to get near it. From a walk it would change to a trot, and then to a swift lope, and presently there would be a straightaway run of fifty or a hundred mules and a calf elk for several miles, a turn, and as frantic a run back. Then how the wagon boss would "cuss" and swear vengeance on the little thing.

No doubt all wild animals know when they cross the fresh trail of a man, but few of them seem to fear it, and many will walk along it. I remember, though, an exception, and that was in the case of a mountain goat, generally conceded to be the most stupid of all game animals. We had traversed a high, steep ridge, my friend and I, and arriving at the end of it sat down to rest. In a few moments we saw an old billygoat slowly making his way up from below, stopping for a bite of some tempting vegetation here and there, never once looking about or sniffing the air to detect the presence of some enemy, as is the habit of the bighorn and deer. But when he struck our trail he bent his head, smelled of it, and then bounded ponderously straight up in the air, a most amusing, ungainly looking beast. When he came down he sniffed the trail once more, and then lumbered away as fast as he could to the opposite end of the ridge and up the steep mountain. I doubt if that goat had ever seen a man, or heard a rifle shot, for we were in an exceedingly wild country, yet he showed more fear of the mere trail of man than any other animal I saw.

The night closed in, the bitterly cold north wind shrieked through the tree tops, and occasional flurries of hard snow rattled down upon the tent roof. Old Cold Maker had at last succeeded in beating back the warm Chinook winds. We feared that winter had come, and retired, expecting, and dreading, to find the river frozen over in the morning.

XI

WE were awakened by a grinding and rasping along the shore, and looking out saw that the river was covered with great cakes of congealed mush ice — more ice than there was open water. There was half an inch of snow on the ground; the wind was still in the north, but the fog had disappeared and the dark gray clouds were scudding along high above the rim of the valley. It was an ideal day for still-hunting, but there was no thought of that now. Here we were, seventy-five miles or more south of the Great Northern Railway, on the south side of the river, and we knew not how many miles from a ranch and a team to take us north to the railroad.

We had a hurried breakfast, loaded the boat, and pushed out into the stream. Here and there among the great floating cakes of ice there was an open lane of water on which I could make good time, and then for a long time we would be inclosed and surrounded, and there was nothing to do but drift until another piece of water opened a way. Geese were unusually numerous; likely they thought it too cold to continue their flight to the south, and they looked rather forlorn as they sat huddled up on the bars. Nevertheless they always flew before we came within range of them, generally lighting a short distance downstream, only to rise and fly on again at our approach, and ere long there were hundreds of them keeping ahead of us, our vanguard as it were. Our friends the sharptail grouse were also in evidence, perched by dozens in the brush and scattering trees along the shores, their necks drawn in, their feathers distended.

A couple of miles below our island camp we passed over McGonnigal's Bar, a bit of river full of sandbars and sand islands; the channel was easily followed, however, as the more rapidly moving ice in it pointed out the way, and we went through without once touching bottom. The bar was named after R. L. McGonnigal, an old friend of ours, who had a woodyard here in the early '70's, and whose remains now lie in the cemetery at Fort Benton. He was born, I believe, in Georgia, lived in Alabama for a time, was an officer in the Confederate army and came to Montana at the close of the war. A kind, genial, whole-souled fellow was Mac. Peace to his shades.

At the foot of the bar we came in sight of the Round Butte, one of the well-known and peculiar landmarks along the river. It stands on a sloping ridge, about a mile south of the stream, and is perfectly cone shaped, its sharp summit surmounted by a few stunted pines. The Blackfeet have two names for it—Heart Butte, the Black Butte. In other days it was a favorite resort of war parties, for from its summit a fine view of the valley may be seen for many miles, both above and below it. And now we began to see the end of the long and all but treeless canyon we had been passing through. Below the butte the valley widens out, and there are large groves of cottonwood on every bottom. We slipped along past the butte, sometimes rowing, but more often drifting with the ice. By this time Sah-né-to was getting thoroughly chilled, although she had on numerous heavy wraps, and I began looking for a camp ground.

We passed a long stretch of timber on the north side, but there was a shallow bar in front of it, and found a place at last on the south side, four miles below the butte. It was two o'clock, and we had come only twelve or thirteen miles since early morning, but I was about worn out with my struggle to row faster than the ice was running. All along Sah-né-to had been "making medicine," addressing most earnest supplications to a certain ancient coyote who was supposed to have great influence over Ai-sto-yi-stam, the Cold Maker, and other gods of the storms and winds. Shortly after we had set up the tent, lo, the clouds broke away, the sun shone warmly and a still warmer Chinook wind began to blow from the west. In half an hour the snow had all disappeared. "See, now, you unbeliever," said Sah-né-to, "the result of my prayers; the gods took pity on us and have brought the warm wind to our aid."

I was up before daylight the next morning. There was still some mush ice in the river, but I had no difficulty in rowing across to the other side. Here was a broad sandbar under a very high cut bank, all cut up by the footprints of deer. Above was the long grove of cottonwoods we had passed the day before, and half a mile below a still larger, wider grove. I bent my steps toward the latter, in hopes of finding something worth shooting at. I traversed the foot of the cut bank a quarter of a mile or more, and then at the mouth of a coulee found a place where I could climb it, up a path several feet in depth, worn by the sharp hoofs of the deer. The moon was shining, and although the sky was beginning to redden in the east, there was not yet sufficient light to enable me to see a deer, so I sat down on the edge of the cut bank and waited fifteen or twenty minutes. Downstream a ways the river bore in sharply against the bank, and as I sat there a large cottonwood which had been undermined toppled in with a reverberating splash, another warning to keep away from the treacherous banks.

I arose and moved on toward the grove a few steps at a time, following the trail which was as plain and hard beaten as any game path I ever saw. Arrived at a clump of trees standing several hundred yards out from the main growth, I stood with my back to one, and as it got lighter I saw seven deer feeding among the sagebrush out at the edge of the bottom. Just beyond them there was a long steep bank, then a bench several hundred yards wide, and then began the steep slope of the hills.

By making a detour down through the timber to where it bordered the steep bank, and then circling up along the flat, I thought I might get within range of them. But I had not gone more than two hundred yards when the willows and rosebrush bordering the wood seemed to be alive with fleeing deer, their white waving tails showing plainly in every direction for a second or two as they leaped into the shelter of the grove. There were bucks and does and fawns, twenty-five or thirty of them, and one old buck must needs lope along an opening, running toward the river. A bullet from my .30-30 caught him in the stern, he stopped, wobbled and fell, and a moment later I had the knife into him. He was a very large, fat old fellow, the primest kind of meat. I looked to see what had become of the seven I had first discovered, and saw them alternately trotting and walking up the long slope into the hills, evidently not very much alarmed.

Of course I hurried back to camp and we had some fried liver and brains for breakfast. After the dishes were washed and everything put in shape about the camp, I determined to pass the day exploring around a bit. The sun was shining brightly, the Chinook wind continued, and there was no more sign of approaching winter save the still passing but lessening flow of ice. Sah-né-to said she felt like having a good long tramp, too, so we crossed the river and set forth.

All along the edge of the timber below where my buck lay, the rose and buck brush was criss-crossed by numberless game trails. A fresh mound of leaves, brush, fallen branches and loose earth attracted our attention, and we found that the uneaten part of a freshly killed deer had been carried up by a grizzly. There were its tracks, made during the night, and they were as large as any footprints of bear I ever saw. At first I feared that the old fellow had been alarmed by my shot in the early morning, but we found his trail going up toward the breaks, and made sure that he had walked along in the game path in the usual slow and deliberate manner of his kind.

As we approached the hills, trail after trail branched off from the main one, and that too soon came to an end, and before us was the hard, grassy slope where not even the sharp hoofs of a deer could leave a mark, and there we lost the tracks of the bear. We kept on, ascending after a little a long, narrow ridge between two deep coulees, and there the grass and other vegetation ended. The top of the backbone was bare, black baked badland. Again we found numberless tracks of deer, and the trails of several bears, old and recent, but not the trail of the deer killer. The coulee down to our right was broad and grassy, and from it lesser ones branched off up into the ridge. In each one of these, and especially on the northeast slopes were small groves of pine, thickets of plum trees. An ideal place for mule deer, I thought, and I was not a little surprised to see a couple of whitetail bucks bound out of the first one we approached. They were within easy range, and likely I could have killed one or both of them, but we had already plenty of meat, and I forebore to shoot, although I longed to do so.

I don't know how long that coulee is; we kept on the ridge above it, even ascending, for four or five miles, but never came to the end of it. At last the divide began to rise in benches, with cliffs of hard sandstone, beneath them belts of fir. Sah-né-to was getting tired, so we concluded to go no further.

It seemed to be a day of big tracks, for at the foot of one of the cliffs we saw the largest bighorn footprints I every ran across. At first I thought they must have been made by an elk, but after following them a ways I was convinced that they really were those of a ram. I would have given much to have seen that animal. A pair of nineteen-inch horns were once found in this country, and I doubt not this particular old ram had a monstrously large pair.

On our way up we had seen five bucks, all whitetail, but no mule deer, nor was there much sign of the latter. Now, the whitetail deer are generally supposed to live almost entirely in the thick timber and willows of the river bottoms, and so do the does and fawns, but my own experience is that the bucks generally take to the hills and pine groves at daylight, returning to the vicinity of the river at dusk, or a little later. At least this is the case along the Missouri. Of course the bucks do remain in the timber of the bottoms, to some extent during the daytime, but the majority take to the hills. If by so doing they imagine they are safer, then their instinct is wrong. The country is so broken that the hunter can generally surprise them in their beds, and obtain a fair running shot at them before they can get over the nearest knoll. And he who cannot take the fall out of one at a hundred yards or so, deserves to live on bacon straight.

We went down into the wide coulee, crossed it, and gradually gaining the top of the next point followed it toward the river. Again on the east side of the ridge we found scattering pine groves, and started two more bucks out of them, but still there was no further sign of the old grizzly. A smaller one had recently crossed the ridge, and there were the deep indentations of another one, made when there had been a heavy rain. I imagine it would be severe work for a bear to wade through this clayey soil in the wet season, sinking into the mud six or eight inches at every step, and carrying sticky masses of it on his paws.

Keeping on top of the ridge, we followed it to the end, then down into the bottom, striking the lower end of the timber in which I had killed the buck. It was useless to hunt for the bear in there, as the fallen leaves were very noisy underfoot.

The deer trails through the bordering rose and buck brush afforded a good and silent path, and we followed them slowly, scanning every bit of the woodland we could see. Poking along this, we saw something looming up in the brush ahead of us and found that it was a Red River cart, one of those massive, high, two-wheeled affairs used by the Cree half-bloods. It had evidently been in good order when left by its owners, but was now checked and warped by the weather. The wrappings, or rather tires of the wheels, were of buffalo rawhide, to which the hair still clung, faded to a brownish white color, but still curly and kinky. Near the cart there were the charred ends of some sticks, an old brass kettle such as the Hudson's Bay Company used to handle, and some buffalo bones.

Why the cart should have been abandoned here was a conundrum, for the Cree half-bloods valued the creaking affairs as highly as a rancher does his wagon. Perhaps its owners were here beset by a war party of Blackfeet, or other Indians, and killed or driven away, and if such was the case, we give the Indians credit for having done one good deed. Riel himself rode in one of these carts. "Do you know," he said to me one day, "Do you know that I compare myself to the David of the Bible? Yes, like him, I am the leader of a persecuted people. Riding in my cart over the plains I am in the habit of composing verses, something like the Psalms. Let me repeat a few of them to you. I would like to get your opinion on the metre."

"Excuse me," I replied, "I am very busy just now mixing some alcohol for your people," and for many a day I avoided him.

We sat down by the cart and ate our lunch. The sight of it brought up many memories of old times and of those queer people, the Cree half-bloods, or more properly, French half-breeds. I can see them yet trailing over the prairie after the buffalo, a string of horses and carts a mile or two long, each one driven by a black-dressed woman or girl, who invariably wore a black silk handkerchief tied over her head. We sold great numbers of them at the rate of a head and tail robe per handkerchief. That was the one article of adornment affected by the women.

The men wore gaudy sashes. How they hated us Americans and the English, calling us heretical dogs, and worse, when they thought we did not understand their bastard French. I was on several buffalo runs with the men. Always, when a herd was sighted, they dismounted, knelt on the plain, and prayed for a successful and safe run, crossing themselves and bowing repeatedly. And the next moment they were up and away, cursing horribly as they urged their horses on. And after they had strewn the plain with the dark brown carcasses of the buffalo, they tried to steal the animals from each other, and there was more cursing, and even fights. And yet, withal, they were arrant cowards, not nearly so brave and determined as the full-blooded Indians.

It was past three o'clock when we came to our buck, having seen nothing of the bear. I cut the deer in two, hung up the forequarters, and carried the balance to the boat, and then to camp. I wanted that bear. After dinner I crossed the river again, and taking a position near its cache, sat and watched and hoped for a sight of the old fellow. As dusk came on some deer appeared here and there along the edge of the timber, some of them gradually feeding out toward the hills, but bruin came not. I waited until it was too dark to see the sights of the rifle plainly, and then sneaked back to the boat and rowed across to camp.

"Have you noticed," Sah-né-to asked, "the broad gashes on the trees here and over where we were today?"

Indeed I had. Forty feet above the summer level of the river the cottonwoods had been scarred by ice during a jam, owing to the sudden breaking up of the river. The months of

December and January in the winter of 1879~80 were bitterly cold, and the river froze to the depth of three feet. The snow was also deep, especially up at the foot of the Rockies. It was, I believe, the 18th of February that an exceedingly warm and furious Chinook wind set in, and soon every coulee on the plains and in the foothills was a running river.

A day or two later a great volume of water swelled the Missouri and tore up the ice, ripping its way along with a tremendous crashing and grinding. Every little way the ice would jam and pile up, twenty, thirty, forty and more feet in height, and the water would back up and spread out over the bottoms seeking new channels, carrying with it the jagged ice which tore up the ground and underbrush, and in places cut in two or carried away large trees. And then with a deafening roar the jam would break and let out the awful flood of water, ice, and debris, only to stop and pile up again a short distance further down the stream. It jammed just below our post, which was thirty feet above the river, and in five minutes the water was four feet deep in the buildings, and but that it soon broke the place must have been swept away.

We had just time to run to the hills, and there we stood, shivering, expecting to see everything carried down the stream. In the warehouse nearly two thousand robes were wet and had to be retanned. Of a pile of sugar, nothing was left but the sacks, and many other goods were ruined. Cottontail rabbits and prairie dogs in the bottoms were well nigh exterminated; deer were killed by hundreds, and many buffalo were caught by the freshet. Even the beaver were drowned out, and in many cases crushed by the ice.

Few people knew that here in the badlands lying south of the Round Butte and between it and the Musselshell, a small herd of buffalo ranged until three years ago. They were the very last of the great northern herds, some thirty-five head, and the country they roamed was so wild, so difficult of access, that the men who knew they were there hoped that they would thrive and increase. These were the great cattle owners of the far-away Judith Basin, whose herds roamed the range for several hundred miles in every direction. Each spring they sent their cowboys into this rough country to drive out the cattle to their branding corrals, and when the buffalo were discovered the word was given that no employee was to kill or molest them under pain of something much worse than the loss of a job. When first found, there were only eighteen head of the buffalo, and part of them were bulls. But year by year the little herd increased, until there were thirty-five, counting calves. And then?

Why those worthless, sneaking scavengers of the plains, the French half-breeds, in some way learned of their existence. Perhaps some cowboy in his cups made known the fact. The word spread. Down came the tattered lodges of the camp at Lewistown, away up in the Judith country, and a slow-moving column of creaking carts, drawn by skinny cayuses, started out for the slaughter. And it was complete. Riding the high ridges, scanning the broken country from the tops of the tall buttes, the scouts finally found the little herd. There was to be no chasing, no old-time run, because by that method some few might escape. Signals were waved back to the on-coming column, the hunters, Baptiste and Bogard, Bonapart, Seviere, and all the rest came hurrying up on their scrawny ponies, cautiously made the surround, closed in, and slaughtered every one of the animals. Alas! Alas! Of little use are our game laws so long as these Canadian breeds are allowed to remain in the State. There is talk of rounding them up and driving them back across the international line. Let us all do what we can to forward that much-desired end.

When the night settled down over the valley, several bands of wolves began their evening chorus, and the owls in the trees about joined in. Sah-né-to does not like owls; they are not birds, according to her philosophy, but the reincarnation of deceased "medicine men," and prone to do serious mischief to us poor mortals.

XII

SOMETIME during the night Sah-né-to awoke me and declared in shrill whispers that she had heard a bear prowling around the tent. We listened for further proof of his presence. There was a thick mat of crisp, new-fallen leaves on the little island, and presently we heard them crackling under the tread of some large animal. I arose and went to the doorway of the tent with my rifle, and stood for some time trying to get a glimpse of the night wanderer in the darkness. Around and about, now to one side and now the other side of the island, it prowled along with slow, soft tread, crushing and shuffling the dead leaves, occasionally breaking a small dry twig. I was satisfied that it was not a deer, for the sound of their sharp hoofs was long since familiar to my ear. Finally the animal left the timber, and I heard it wading through the shallow slough which at this part of the dry island separated us from the main shore, and then all was quiet. I had a smoke, waiting, and shivering in the cold air, to hear its footsteps again, and hearing nothing, finally returned to bed and slept soundly until morning.

Not so Sah-né-to; hour after hour she lay listening for, and dreading the return of the animal, and at daylight again awakened me, and we had our breakfast. As soon as the meal was over I crossed the river in the boat, Sah-né-to accompanying me, and took my previous position to watch the big grizzly's cache. The sun came up, several hours passed, but he did not appear, and we went back to camp. Perhaps he had killed, or found another deer, or more likely, in some way we had alarmed him.

After washing the dishes and getting camp in presentable shape, we started across the bottom and up the breaks, which are in this vicinity exceedingly rough. Crossing the bar between the island and the main shore, we passed close to the slough and found the tracks of the disturber of our rest; and sure enough it had been a bear. There were its tracks plain and sharp in the wet sand, and they were grizzly tracks of good size. "Ah!" said Sah-né-to, "now do you believe me? You declared that what we heard was merely the hopping of a rabbit upon the dead leaves, but I knew all the time that you were only saying that to quiet my fears."

It was perhaps a mile and a half up to the foot of the sandstone cliffs and buttes forming the rim of the valley. On our way up we saw several mule deer, and, arrived at the base of a high broken cliff, we discovered a nice bunch of bighorn feeding along its crest. We found a place, a game trail worn along the side of a rocky slope, which enabled us to ascend to the top. The sheep had disappeared, and we went on further, ascending a little butte, from the summit of which we obtained a magnificient view of that weird and wonderful badland country. Hundreds of buttes were in sight, pyramidal, flat-topped, trunk-shaped, some of them showing only the bare earth, others grass grown, some fairly well timbered; and stretching away toward the Yellowstone were the timbered gashes and the rough breaks of Paradise, or Little Snow Creek, which enters the Missouri five miles below the Round Butte. I have been unable to learn when or why this little stream received its peculiar names. Undoubtedly it was once a paradise for the red hunter, its willow-margined banks, its little grassy flats and its rough timbered breaks teeming with game—the buffalo, the elk, the deer, antelope and mountain sheep. The buffalo and elk have now disappeared, of course, but of the others goodly numbers still drink of its alkaline water.

The day was pleasant, a clear sky and a warm west wind, and we sat on the top of the butte several hours taking in the wonderfully grand and weird scenery. "Oh!" said Sah-né-to, at last, "why could it not have lasted? Why did the white people rob us of our happy life? Why could we not have always lived the life for which Old Man created us? We had the buffalo, which were not only food, but clothing and shelter; and we wandered at will over hundreds of miles of these plains and mountains. And now, the game is nearly gone, the buffalo have all disappeared, and my people will shortly share their fate. Year by year, hemmed in upon a reservation, living upon scanty food which the Great Father furnishes them, they are passing rapidly away."

"Yes, Sah-né-to," I said, "your words are true. The whites have deprived your people of their free and happy life. Yet, had they never come to this country, we would never have met."

"Ai, that also is true; my heart is divided. I love my people with a part of it, but the greater part is yours. You have been good and kind to me always. Oh! but the pitifulness of it all. Last winter, you remember, we went to Great Falls by the narrow-track railway, and we crossed the Bear River at Fort Conrad. You remember how it used to be when we lived there so many years ago, the happy children playing upon the ice, spinning their tops and sliding upon it, and the men and women crossing back and forth? And last winter, when I saw the frozen, desolate stream, I remembered those days and mourned. They are gone, the most of those happy people; few are left, and they sit in sadness and want, awaiting the end. Soon the last one of them will be gone, and the name of my people will be but a memory. Alas! Alas!"

We finally started for camp, the dinner hour beginning to assert itself. We saw more mountain sheep, more deer, and a band of antelope going down to the river for water; but we had plenty of meat, and I forebore to shoot at any of them.

In the evening, after a satisfying meal, I again crossed the river and watched a while for the big grizzly to appear at his cache. But he did not come. At sunset the deer stole out of the thick timber and fed along its edge. Some of them within easy rifle shot, but they were not what I sought, and I went home in the gathering darkness without having fired a shot.

We had a slight lunch, and prepared to retire at nine o'clock. About that time the wind changed, and a bitterly cold blast swept into the valley from the north. Sah-né-to said that the Cold Maker had arrived.

And she was right; when we arose in the morning the river was full of floating ice cakes, and the shore was lined by a broad fringe of it. All hope of finding the big grizzly, or other of his kin, was given up. We were certain that winter had come, and that our only chance to get to the mouth of Milk River and the railroad was to start at once. After a hurried breakfast we struck camp, loaded the Good Shield, and pushed out into the stream. The water was fairly swift, and we soon ran by the mouth of Paradise Creek. The timbered bottom at its confluence with the river is several miles long, and shelters many a deer. As we went on under sail and oar, crushing through the ice cakes, the bottoms became wider and more heavily timbered. After an eight-mile struggle we passed Hell Creek, so named, as an old friend told me, "because a man always has a hell of a time to cross it horseback, owing to its cut banks and treacherous bottom." From there a further run of four miles took us to Featherland Island, and the mouth of Wolf Creek, which comes in from the north.

The island was named after old Bill Featherland, an employee of the American Fur Company. He wintered upon it in the season of 1859–60, and killed, poisoned and trapped fifteen hundred wolves, to say nothing of coyotes and kit foxes. From all accounts, Featherland was a gruff, quick-tempered man, who never failed to say just what he thought. Once at Fort Union he was in the carpenter shop at work when a steamboat arrived having on board some Jesuit priests. One of these, wandering around, entered the place and said, in his broken English, "Company shop? Company shop?"

"Yes," Bill replied, "company shop."

After a little another priest came in and asked the same question.

"Yes," Bill replied, turning angrily upon him, "Company shop. How many times do you want me to tell you so? Git out of here."

The priest ran out as fast as his long robe would allow him to, crying, "Bad man. Bad man. Help! Help!"

On we went, as fast as we could push through the congealing cakes of mush ice, which scraped and cut the bow of the Good Shield like a knife. Down past Anna Island, past Flirt Creek and Willow Island, and then we turned northward into Red Cloud Bend. The north wind was sharp, the current swift, and an appalling sea was running. I lowered the sail and took the oars. Sah-né-to crouched in the stern, covering her eyes with her hands, trembling with fright, but making no complaint except to once say, "Surely the water spirits will now claim us for their own."

I will admit that I was also scared; the skiff plunged into wave after wave, taking water every time, and there were, it seemed, a thousand snags to be avoided. At last, however, we reached the northern end of the bend, under the shelter of a high cut bank, and ran into still water. Sah-né-to vowed a gift to the sun for our preservation.

This bend is where the *Red Cloud*, that best of river boats, sunk in 1884. The stream is full of sawyers, and during such a gale as we had experienced the boat, heavily loaded and headed upstream, was pierced by one, sinking in a few moments, fortunately without loss of life. The shifting sands have long since covered her, no part of her remaining in sight.

Passing the bend, the wind again favored us, and we sailed along at a good clip in spite of the ice. We passed, three miles below the bend, the bottom where we had conducted a branch trading post in days gone by, but I did not stop to review the familiar place. And then we sailed by the mouth of the Little Dry Fork, and an hour later camped for the night on the shore of Flopping Bill's Bottom, named after that murderous leader of the gang which has previously been mentioned. The shore was covered with deer tracks, and as we went into the brush to select a place for the tent, we saw several waving tails vanishing through the willows.

The wind went down at dusk, but the night was cold, and there was more ice drifting down in the morning than on the previous day. It is a mystery to me how we made the thirty-eight miles to the mouth of Milk River that day, but we did so, landing at the mouth of the sluggish stream at dusk, within sight and sound of the trains of the Great Northern Railway. In the morning I hired an Indian boy to take us out to the station, and we reluctantly parted with the Good Shield, which had been to us such a staunch and serviceable craft. We gave it to the boy who took us out to the station.

And thus ended the most pleasant of the many trips Sah-né-to and I have taken, and we vowed to repeat it another year.*

*They never again floated the Missouri together; Sah-né-to died within a year.

INDEX